MW01635385

John & Andrea
Enjoy
Mother & Dad.

W. J. OLIVER

Life Through a Master's Lens

by
Sheilagh S. Jameson

Glenbow Museum
1984

ISBN 0-919224-39-3

Dedicated to Marjorie B. Oliver

This publication pays tribute to the centennial of Banff National Park and the national parks system, 1885–1985.

Contents

Cavvy on roundup near Hussar

Preface

During the years that W. J. Oliver's career flourished, his name was well known across Canada and in international circles. His work received wide distribution and despite the fact that much of it did not bear his name there was recognition of his outstanding ability as a nature and action photographer. Newspapers highlighted many of his activities and various articles in periodicals recorded some of his experiences.

From my home on a ranch at Millarville near the Oliver's Diamond L Ranch, I was aware from the mid-thirties onward of the drama surrounding W. J. Oliver's life, and, vicariously, of the excitement of his frequent homecomings and departures on photographing expeditions. I had the privilege of viewing films shown in his home or at local gatherings, of listening to his incomparable commentaries, and experiencing the vitality and dynamism of his presence. Even then I was aware that here was a fascinating saga which should be recorded.

Research for this biography was commenced in 1981 and certain factors key to Bill Oliver's career quickly became clear—his boundless energy and drive, his individualistic approach to undertakings, his amazing productivity, and the excellence and unique quality of his work. I realized, too, that his wife's encouragement and her ability to oversee management of both studio and ranch during his absences enabled him to attain his position of eminence among Canada's camera men. W. J. Oliver became one of the most noted outdoor photographers of his day and he left a legacy of pictorial work which has stood the test of time.

The production of this book would not have been possible without the co-operation and assistance of Mrs. Marjorie B. Oliver and her three daughters, Joan Cavers, Doreen Huffman, and Audrey-Jean Langford. They were most generous in providing information and access to relative manuscript and photographic material. I express my very warm and sincere thanks to each of them. My gratitude also is extended to Duncan Cameron, Glenbow Museum's Director, for his interest and support; to Hugh A. Dempsey, Assistant Director (Collections), who is in charge of Glenbow's publication program, for editing the manuscript and making publication arrangements; to members of the Archives and Library for their customary cheerful helpfulness, particularly Georgeen Klassen whose aid in selecting photographs was invaluable; and, also, to the Photographic Department for co-operation and expertise in the production of prints.

I am indebted, also, to other institutions: the Archives of the Canadian Rockies; Public Archives of Canada, notably the National Film, Television and Sound Archives and the division of the National Photography Collection; the Provincial Archives of British Columbia and David Mattison for his continued help; the CPR Archives; and the Nova Scotia Museum. In addition, individuals who knew Bill Oliver kindly supplied information and confirmed relative data. These included: W. Fergus Lothian, Ottawa, historian of Parks Canada; W. M. (Toppy) Edwards, Arizona; E. J. (Bud) Cotton, Calgary; and E. Walter Cadman, Calgary. To these and others I express deep gratitude for their assistance and their interest.

Grants from the Archdeacon Swanson Fund and the Explorations Program of the Canada Council made possible necessary data gathering trips and covered other research expenses. In addition the Exhibition Program of Canada Council provided assistance to the Glenbow Museum for the mounting of an exhibition featuring W. J. Oliver's work and for the simultaneous publication of this work.

SHEILAGH S. JAMESON

Maligne Lake at the Narrows, ca.1929. This was one of Oliver's most widely circulated photographs.

I. An Epic Moment

Bill Oliver rechecked the lists and notes before him. He was a man well accustomed to planning trips. Making preparations for spending a week or two photographing mountain climbers in the Rockies, or getting ready for longer journeys in the national parks across Canada—these activities had become a part of his career. However, the plans now represented by the papers on his desk dealt with something quite different: the prospect of a four-month expedition photographing big game hunting in Africa. It was crucial there be no mistakes or omissions in planning.

He had written to sources in England for information, and to the Eastman Kodak people in New York concerning photography in the tropics and the care of film there. Tin boxes especially made for packing and carrying film were ready for him in New York. They were designed to maintain the correct humidity, blotting paper being one substance used for the purpose. Then there was a slow motion camera to pick up in New York, and the large quantity of film he required. Michael Lerner, the leader and instigator of the expedition, was putting through an order for supplies and a telegram from him requested information on quantities of film needed, both colour and black and white, and discussed relative use of 16 and 35 mm.[1] Telegrams from New York came almost daily to the Oliver Studio in Calgary and phone calls from Lerner were a common occurrence.[2]

Bill Oliver felt that luck had played an important part in bringing him to the brink of this African expedition. Just a few months earlier during the summer of 1936 he had undertaken an assignment in the Maritimes for the National Parks Branch of Canada. This included the taking of promotional pictures for the newly-formed Cape Breton Highlands National Park, making a series of photographs along the Cabot Trail to publicize the highlights and picturesque beauty of this scenic route in anticipation for a national park in Prince Edward Island,[3] and the production of a photographic record of the ruins of the old Fortress of Louisbourg.[4] One cloudy and rainy day, conditions were not conducive to picture taking so Bill set off for a drive through the Nova Scotian countryside. Coming to a crossroads he was undecided which route to take, so he settled the matter by flipping a coin. Following the road to the east, as indicated by this toss of fortune, he presently found himself in Louisbourg.

The town seemed deserted but he soon discovered the townspeople on the wharf where a state of rare excitement prevailed: a huge broadbill swordfish weighing 462 pounds had just been landed.[5] The fisherman, Michael Lerner, was a member of the Cape Breton Expedition of the American Museum of Natural History, headed by Dr. J. T. Nicholls, which had been formed primarily to study the swordfish. Bill joined the admiring crowd and having a natural sensitivity to news stories, he approached Lerner and requested permission to photograph the expedition's next swordfishing venture.

Lerner, widely recognized for his prowess as fisherman and hunter, was the millionaire owner of the Lerner dress shops which flourished in a series of major American cities. Every day he was approached by supplicants with a variety of requests and he had developed an understandable wariness. The man before him, however, was obviously someone to consider. He was a vigorous outdoors type, of medium height and athletic build, handsome with thick black hair, his youthful appearance belying his forty-nine years. He had a direct open look, his brown eyes reflecting interest and enthusiasm, and there was about him a certain air of vitality and inner force. Still, with the caution born of experience Michael Lerner hesitated, so Bill suggested thay they phone a representative of the Parks Branch who would verify his credentials. This they did and shortly thereafter Bill Oliver prepared to go on the forthcoming fishing trip. He left the next day for a quick return to Sydney to attend to business matters there, then on 9 August he set out from Louisbourg with the swordfishing expedition.

The Canadian Government vessel, *Margaret SII*, under the command of Captain George Myra, served as an off-shore mother ship for the fishing party. Once a rum runner plying these coastal seas, the vessel's present more mundane duty still was not without exciting moments, as the expedition was

William J. Oliver

to prove. The *Margaret* cruised the waters in search of swordfish and on the morning of 12 August when some forty miles out in the Atlantic a broadbill was sighted. The actual fishing was not done from the *Margaret*. Rather, a dory with an outboard motor under fishing guide Captain Tom Gifford and mate Larry Bagby was launched and soon the big fish had taken the bait on Lerner's line. After a fight of one hour and 29 minutes, a swordfish weighing 535 pounds was brought aboard. This, however, was just the start of the venture as less than two hours later another broadbill came into view. Again, Lerner went out in the dory. Shortly a giant swordfish was on his line and he was engaged in one of the fiercest fishing battles of his career. He was seated in a specially constructed swivel chair equipped with strong footrests and firmly mounted in the dory. As the huge fish lunged and struggled, the small craft in tow was tossed and flung over some twelve miles of sea while the boatmen worked desperately to keep it afloat. The battle lasted for four hours and two minutes, the victory going eventually to the man. The sea creature weighing 601 pounds, measuring thirteen feet six inches in length and five feet six inches in girth, proved to be the largest swordfish ever caught off the North Atlantic coast. Lerner had set a further record as the first man to catch two swordfish in one day on the Atlantic.[6]

During the fight the *Margaret* had followed the combatants, coming in as closely as possible to the action, while Bill Oliver kept cranking his camera, pausing only to reload film. The movie he produced was an excellent record of a unique story. Later, he sent a copy to Lerner in accordance with arrangements made by the Parks Department. The fisherman was delighted; through the film he could relive this event, for the turmoil of action, the fierceness of the struggle, the feel— it was all there.[7]

Bill Oliver continued with his work in the Maritimes but then was asked to photograph a Lerner tuna fishing trip off Shelbourne, Nova Scotia. By 30 August, he was out in Jordan Bay filming. Lerner used a rod and reel as opposed to the traditional harpooning done by commercial fishermen, a method of tuna fishing which he and Kip Farrington had pioneered in 1935,[8] and succeeded in catching some big ones. Again Bill produced an exciting action-packed movie.[9]

By now the American sportsman had developed a genuine liking for the photographer so when plans were underway for Lerner's big game hunting expedition to Africa late that fall, he was most anxious that W. J. Oliver should join the party as official photographer.

Upon Bill's return from the Maritimes, his wife, Marjorie and their three daughters drove in from the ranch at Millarville to meet him at the station. Meetings such as this were a part of the pattern of their lives. With happy, excited chatter the

Harbour in the Maritimes, 1936

family gathered up his baggage and equipment and headed for home. They were well along on their thirty-two mile drive into the foothills when, during a slight lull, Bill said, "What would you think if I went to Africa on a trip?"[10] The family gave him their immediate and complete attention, the girls sitting on the edge of the back seat and craning forward to catch every word. He had to tell him the whole story. Joan, the eldest, at fifteen had been on some of her father's photographing trips and had some appreciation of what this opportunity meant to him as a photographer. Nevertheless, she and her sisters, Doreen aged thirteen and Audrey-Jean (or A.J.) just ten, were aware of how much they would miss him. A.J., an intense child who worried about her adventuresome father, was quite frightened by the prospect. She had read of Africa as "the dark continent" and her active mind conjured up terrifying pictures of fierce jungle animals and equally ferocious cannibalistic natives. However, despite A.J.'s frightening visions and worse nightmares, the girls were caught up in their father's excitement over the trip. His wife Marjorie also knew the dangers but curbing her fears, she agreed wholeheartedly to the trip.

The new experience and professional opportunity were not the only reasons why Bill Oliver wished to go on the African expedition; he felt it was too good a financial enterprise to miss. During the Great Depression, when studio photography suffered, he had to avail himself of every opportunity of adding to his income. He had been fortunate enough in having continued work with the National Parks Branch, particularly as the outdoor photography involved appealed to him. With stills he could interpret Nature's beauty, ruggedness, artistry; with movies he could interpret action, record achievements, capture something of the movements of wild animals at home. Certainly at times there was danger; he had shot pictures from positions ranging from insecure to downright perilous and encountered dangerous animals including stampeding buffalo and ferocious grizzlies. But he constantly took chances because of his desire to get good shots.

Bill had persuaded Marjorie to take the girls to England for the four months of his absence so soon all members of the family were busy making preparations for the trip. The plan was that the family should all travel together by train to Montreal, then Marjorie and the girls would sail for England. Bill could look after their embarkation arrangements, see them aboard the *Duchess of Richmond*, and then go south to New York.

Just before they left Alberta, as Bill Oliver drove to the ranch, his mind was busy with all the household and ranch matters he had to attend to before leaving. His foreman would look after the ranch. The house would be closed so he would have to take the batteries of the Delco light system into Calgary, otherwise they would freeze. He mentally ticked off various ranch affairs that he should discuss with his foreman. Then his thoughts turned to his old home at Ash, England. He had made many trips back, and always it was good to see the old place again and to be welcomed by his mother and brother, Reg. It was twenty-seven years since he had first left home bound for a young developing land, adventure, and a new life. Things had not worked as he had planned; there had been some ups and downs, and fate had taken a hand at times. In fact, the route he had followed was better than the one he had sought. They had been good years, the active, eventful ones which had brought him to this point in his life.

W. J. Oliver's ranchhouse in winter, 1936

II. The Beginning

William John Oliver was born on 28 July 1887, at Ash in the County of Kent, England, eldest child of Emma Phoebe and Tom Oliver. The home of his birth was a large two-storey house surrounded by fields and orchards—predominately apple and cherry—which his father owned and operated as a fruit and market garden business. Appropriately the house was named "The Orchard." When William John was two years old, another boy, Reginald, was born and in 1894 a little sister named Kathie joined the family briefly; she lived just a year.

William John was always called Will by his mother but outside the family circle, Bill was his usual name and one that seemed more suited to his personality. He and Reginald were very different. Bill was dark haired, out-going, fun-loving and inclined towards mischief, while Reg was fair skinned and more serious and reserved by nature. When they went to children's parties, Bill teased the little girls, pulling hair and sashes, but Reg, a more quiet little boy, behaved with greater propriety.

Ash was a typical English village. Its narrow main street, named High Street, with shops and houses closely fringing its sides, was dominated by the pub and St. Nicholas' Anglican Church. St. Nicholas' was also a dominant factor in the lives of the Oliver boys from early childhood. The family attended church regularly and when Bill became old enough, he provided the boy power required to work the bellows for the church organ. He also had a good voice and sang in the choir for some years, looking deceptively angelic in his choir boys' surplice.

As the Oliver boys grew older and their horizons widened, they became more aware of the Kentish countryside in which they lived. There were fishing villages along the coast, while some sixteen miles from Canterbury the eastern stretch of the North Downs terminated in the white chalk cliffs of Dover. The flavour of the sea was here. The ports of Dover, Hastings, Hythe, Romney, and Sandwich had provided England with naval protection for centuries and into their harbours had come vessels from far across the sea. To a sensitive boy with an ingrained sense of adventure, the winds from the sea carrying the call of distant lands might well have struck a responsive chord. Perhaps they fanned into being a yearning to travel, to see beyond the horizon.

Bill's primary years were spent in the village school in Ash, after which he was sent to Major Mate's Private School. As might be expected, the Major was a martinet who ran his school along military lines. Whether or not young Bill appreciated the strict discipline, he evidently accepted it, but his studies for the most part did not appeal to him. He excelled in rugby and cricket and was attracted to any pursuit connected with the outdoors. He passed examinations with commendable results but by the time he was sixteen he realized that higher learning was not for him. He felt strongly, too, that no type of office or indoor work could bring him satisfaction or happiness. However, the avenue of outside work with which he had had some experience, the orchard and market garden business, was one which he knew definitely he did not want to pursue. There were not many opportunities for a boy seeking employment in Ash at this time, but before long he was apprenticed to William Strachan, butcher in the village.

Young William J. Oliver was pleased to be entering the working world. His duties were varied and provided scope for his energies. He liked making deliveries, as this entailed driving and handling horses and contact with customers. He discovered, too, that the work could offer a number of interests and challenges, so he determined that if butchering was to be his life work, he would be a good butcher. He decided to become truly knowledgeable about cattle so spent extra time studying bovine anatomy and diseases. William Strachan, pleased by the interest and capability of his apprentice, had the boy accompany him when he went to the markets at Canterbury and elsewhere to buy beef animals. Bill made the most of these market sessions, learning what to look for in a good beef animal, what constituted good conformation, how to estimate weight and other elements of stockman's lore.[1]

Some time after Bill had become indoctrinated into the life of a butcher's apprentice, the villagers of Ash became aware of something unusual at the local chemist's shop. Deciding to try

Bill Oliver with his mother and younger brother Reginald, ca.1890

a different form of advertising, the chemist had devised a contest, a decision which was to have unforeseen and far reaching consequences in Bill Oliver's life. In the window displayed among the exotic items which give a chemist's shop an air of mystery, was an ordinary lump of coal. Beside it was a camera, and a notice that it would be given to the person who could guess most closely the weight of the lump of coal.

Bill paused daily in front of the window. It would be great to have a camera; however, every time he looked at that chunk of coal his mind came up with a different weight. At length with characteristic initiative and determination he hit upon a way to lessen the guess work. Obtaining a short length of narrow board, he notched the edges to make a rough gauge, and at the earliest opportunity he returned to the window. As unobtrusively as possible, he extended his arm and sighting along the edge of his gauge, took measurements of the dimensions of the coal, carefully marking the size on the gauge. On arrival home he checked the coal cellar for a lump of coal of appropriate size, which he trimmed to closely approximate the dimensions of the piece in the window; next it was weighed with care. He submitted his estimate and ultimately became the proud possessor of the chemist's camera.

Bill immediately studied the instructions and read all available material on the principles and techniques of taking photographs and developing them. As he had planned, the camera accompanied him on his daily rounds. His employer had secured a contract to supply fresh beef to the army and navy and on delivery trips along the water front he found much to photograph. Soon all his leisure time was spent out with his camera and very early he developed a faculty for recognizing the elements required to make good pictures as opposed to merely shooting photographs. Instinctive, too, was a facility in perceiving and taking potential news pictures. When King Alfonso of Spain arrived in England on the occasion of his betrothal to Queen Victoria's granddaughter, Princess Ena (Victoria Eugenie), Bill Oliver, butcher's apprentice, obtained a good picture of him. Again when the princess left for Spain prior to her marriage on 31 May 1906, Bill managed to take several pictures of her. Similarly on 25 July 1909, he was on hand to photograph Louis Bleriot landing after making the first flight across the English Channel. His concern in taking photographs such as these was the interest of the occasion and the excitement of shooting them, there was no thought of their commercial value. In any case he would not have been able to deliver them to a newspaper in time as all developing was done at home in the evening after the day's work. However, some of his pictures gained local recognition and some small return. On occasion, he produced photographs of first class beef animals intended for the Christmas market and these were retained by stockmen as records, Bill being rewarded by packets of cigarettes for his trouble. The taking of these photographs, however, was of great consequence to the young man. They were his first pictures of animals and through them he discovered the special gratification and thrill of animal photography.[2]

As the years passed, Bill felt more deeply the call of far lands, of adventure. He now had a means of livelihood, butchering, and an interesting hobby, photography. His father intended to will the orchard business to his sons but only Reg seemed to find the enterprise of interest and showed no signs of sharing his brother's urge to roam. At last Bill proposed an agreement: if Reg would remain home and help with the operation of the business, he could in the course of time have complete ownership. Bill, thus freed to travel, would relinquish his share in Reg's favour. This settlement was fair and pleased both boys.

There wasn't much money available to start him off in a new land but Bill was not too concerned about that. He got a third class ticket and early in 1910 sailed from Liverpool on the *Lusitania* bound for New York. He visited his Uncle Austin in New York state and learned that job opportunities in that area also were scarce. His uncle's advice, to go on to western Canada, coincided with his own wishes. Back in Kent he had heard much about Canada, particularly the ranch country of southern Alberta. The stories had fired his imagination and ambition; where there were cattle in such numbers, there should be opportunities for a good butcher. He had heard of a large meat packing firm, Pat Burns and Company, which doubtless would hire another experienced man. He travelled by colonist car to Montreal and then west.[3] The country was so vast, the wooded areas giving place to prairie which stretched in seemingly endless waves. To Bill, however, it was very new and exciting, but he was glad when eventually on 17 April 1910, the train pulled into Calgary.

"NO ENGLISHMAN NEED APPLY"

Calgary in 1910 was a busy, hustling city. It was ambitious with high aspirations, and the exuberant enthusiasm of its promotors blossomed forth in extravagant prose. An eye catching heading in the *Calgary Herald* of 5 March 1910, proclaimed that Calgary was the fastest growing city in Canada. The article following declared that this "City of Sunshine and Opportunity" had, during the past three years, "presented a most marvellous record of growth and development," millions of dollars having been expended "with a view to making it the greatest and most magnificent city of the Middle West." The city's buildings, its educational facilities, its commercial development, and its industrial potential were all extolled.[4]

Certainly the city was riding a wave of prosperity. These were the boom years and real estate was big business. At one juncture in 1910, an acre of undeveloped land in Mount Royal was offered for $4,700, but such bargains did not last long.[5] House and property values varied widely. Two lots with a seven-roomed house, fully modern, together with a three-roomed cottage, a barn and wagon sheds might sell for $7,000; asking prices could run over $9,000, but most houses were advertised for amounts ranging from around $900 to $4,000.[6] Indicative of the market trend is the fact that the land where the York Hotel was later built sold for $12,500 in 1907 and $100,000 in 1910.[7]

As might be expected, in 1910 Calgary was experiencing an invasion of new arrivals and before the end of the year the little city was boasting of a population of 40,000.[8] On 11 April, an immigrant train brought some 300 newcomers, an influx that must have severely taxed the city's facilities; indeed one writer complained that even before the arrival of the train, some individuals were already sleeping on the floor of the depot.[9] These new immigrants and other constant arrivals meant keen competition in the job market. So when Bill Oliver went forth on the morning of 18 April to seek employment, he was confronted with a situation very different from any he had previ-

Looking west on Eighth Avenue, Calgary, in the teens

ously encountered. The job he had so confidently expected to find in the booming little city just was not forthcoming.

There *was* work available. There were openings for a barber, coat maker, harness maker, man with team, clerk with knowledge of typewriting, first class painter, saddlery apprentice; also for carpenters, real estate, and other salesmen, cooks (white), experienced gardeners, cement workers and sidewalk finishers, blacksmiths, teamsters, bushmen, graders, quarrymen, farm hands and sundry others.[10] But there were no requests for workers in the meat business. It soon became obvious to Bill that positions were far outnumbered by the number of applicants and of these "green Englishmen" were most unlikely to be successful. Some places of employment made clear their policy that "no Englishmen need apply,"[11] and Bill Oliver's clothing, speech and fresh-faced appearance clearly indicated that he was newly-arrived from England. At meat packing establishments, Burns included, if he managed to get past the gateman, he was stopped by an overseer or foremen, and no one was impressed by the fact that he had learned the skill of butchering through an apprenticeship in the village of Ash, England.

Actually, although neither Calgary nor young William J. Oliver would be aware of the fact, each possessed qualities of a type to engender an affinity between them. There was about the town and the country it served, an air of energy, vitality and optimism, attributes with which the young Englishman was abundantly endowed. A climate that encouraged entrepreneurship pervaded the town and Bill with his drive, his inborn facility for capitalizing on opportunity, his will to succeed, was surely a prospective entrepreneur. He had the qualities required for achievement and perhaps the atmosphere of the West, and the hard knocks of fortune which revealed the strength of the metal below, helped to develop and coalesce these qualities. Besides an affinity with the hustle of success, Bill with his sense of artistry and love of nature, was atune to the beauty of the western country; its wilderness and rugged grandeur appealed particularly to some feeling deep within him.

But the blossoming of such affinities was in the future. Calgary in 1910 appeared not to be ready to accept the young Englishman—it seemed that he must prove himself first. And this he proceeded to do.

Bill Oliver's remaining money quickly disappeared. He had to get work and was willing to take anything. "Anything" turned out to be two out-of-town jobs that spring and summer. One, rather ironically in view of his feelings regarding the market garden business, was work in the potato fields near Brooks, approximately 110 miles to the south-east of Calgary. The other was more to his liking despite the fact that the hours here, too, were long and the work hard. He managed to convince a prospective employer that he could handle horses and soon he was employed as a teamster on an irrigation project at Strathmore, some 30 miles east of the city. Almost two months later with hardened hands, broadened experience, and a stake of $50, he was back in Calgary in search of a better job. An approach to the P. Burns Company again met with failure; there still seemed to be no place for his butchering skills. No other job of interest seemed available either, so once more Bill Oliver was in the position of having to take any work he could find.

Building in Calgary was still booming so he signed on with a contractor, shovelling gravel and mixing concrete. It was the hardest work he had yet encountered, however, he stayed with it until near the end of 1910, when a shipper for Plunkett and Savage, wholesale dealers in fruit and farm produce, offered him something better. This entailed working long days in the warehouse basement preparing potatoes for retail merchants by removing sprouts, sorting and sacking. He assisted, too, in loading and unloading freight wagons. It was boring work but served as a stopgap measure.

During this rather low period in his life, Bill had the good fortune to meet a young Irish American, Luther McCarty, who was to become a noted pugilist. A warm friendship developed between the two men. Luther, or "Lucky" (usually shortened to "Luck"), had endured a rough life and the various experiences he had encountered made him a person of some standing among men. He had worked on farms and ranches and had done odd jobs around towns; he had travelled to South America, China and Japan as a seaman and had traversed his own country by riding the rails. After some involvement in the boxing business in Culbertson, Montana, he had decided early in 1911 to come north by freight train into Canada. He was a

Calgary Tigers, playing at Hillhurst Park, in the teens

Lacrosse game, Calgary, in the teens

good natured man, warm hearted and generous to a fault, and typically he extended ready friendship to the young Englishman who was struggling to make his way and adapt to the customs of a new land.

In February 1911, McCarty became acquainted with Tommy Burns, head of Calgary's boxing fraternity, with the result that he had the opportunity to participate in a few matches that spring. There was considerable interest in the bouts and promoter Tommy Burns was impressed by the big fighter's ability and style. Bill, who had retained both his interest in photography and his innate sense of the topical, took a picture of Luck poised ready for a fight. This he sold to the *Morning Albertan*.[12] Despite adverse publicity following McCarty's mid-April fight, Burns advised him to go into serious training and shortly after this, the fighter left for Chicago,[13] promising his friend, W.J. and others that he would be back.

Meanwhile, Bill continued with his potato handling job but was alert in seeking opportunities for more congenial employment. He checked the newspapers with care and one April morning in that spring of 1911, while waiting for the warehouse door to open, an advertisement in the *Morning Albertan* caught his eye. It read: "Wanted—Photographer for good paying business; no money required."[14] This appealed to Bill: photography which he regarded as his hobby to be a paying business and without requirement of capital. Leaving the others to load the sacks of potatoes, he rushed off to answer the ad, which had been inserted by Frederick B. Cooper, Photographer, with a studio at 228A - 8th Avenue East.[15] He presented himself as an experienced cameraman and undoubtedly made the most of his past photographic successes. He was hired on the spot.

Bill Oliver spent the next few months as camera assistant at the Cooper studio. His interest in photography had been keen from the time he won the chemist's camera in Ash, and as he learned techniques he had professed to know and gained new facility in the photographic process his enthusiasm for the work grew. His former hobby was now his means of livelihood and was becoming increasingly satisfying. It is a matter of conjecture just when he came to regard photography as a career but even in the 1911 city directory he was listed as a photographer.[16]

After several months at Cooper's, Bill had in all likelihood learned as much as he could in the situation and undoubtedly he had given good service while doing so. Now, however, he was ready for a further challenge. The initiative and enterprise he showed in finding such a challenge indicated the blossoming of his inherent entrepreneurship. In the fall of 1911 he approached the editor of the *Morning Albertan* with the suggestion that his paper was in need of a first class photographer and that he, Bill Oliver, was the man for the job. The editor at this time was William M. Davidson, a man with a reputation for austerity, who was an extremely hard worker himself and liked to have people around him who not only worked hard but enjoyed it.[17] Possibly he recognized this potential in young Oliver; at any rate he agreed to give the idea a try.

The months that followed were exhilarating for the photographer as he roamed the city and its environs and carried out assignments for the paper. From the beginning his main interest lay in sports and outdoor photography and shortly he discovered the special excitement of taking action shots. For example, a high school pole vaulting record was set that fall and an excellent photo of the event caught C. Sinclair, champion, in mid air. This was credited to Turner and Oliver.[18] Some assignments were rather bizarre as on the occasion that the *Albertan* agreed to publish a photograph of a dead man to assist in his identification—Bill took the picture, a crisp close-up.[19] The trips most to his liking were those which he made out in the country where he captured some excellent views of harvest scenes.[20]

At times when money was scarce at the *Albertan* the editor dealt with the situation by giving his photographer drafts for goods on local merchants who owed the paper money for advertising. This meant that Bill lived well and dressed well, even though he sometimes had very little cash.[21] For an ambitious young man, this type of living could not suffice for long, so in 1912 he decided to try a photographic enterprise of his own in addition to his newspaper work.[22] He made arrangements to use space in the basement of the house where he roomed, 314 - 7th Avenue East, for a darkroom and office combined, the first W. J. Oliver Photographic Studio.

He was able to find business from the beginning, undoubtedly his best advertising being by word of mouth and through

Bill Oliver with his Indian motorcycle and camera equipment

the excellence of his product. Having his own business gave him the kind of freedom he desired and this—together with newspaper work which also required considerable personal initiative—provided breadth of scope, thus setting the pattern he would pursue throughout his career.

As Bill Oliver ranged further afield in his work for the *Albertan* he found transportation a problem. Trains did not always run when and where he needed to go. He decided he must have some personal means of travel so in 1912 he bought a motorcycle, a second-hand 'Indian'. Riding was rough on the best of roads on cycles, which lacked balloon tires and spring frames, while on rutted roads and prairie trails it could be really hazardous. When the ruts were deep, he had to fold up the footboards but despite all precautions he and the cycle overturned periodically. The load he carried did not make riding any easier. His large Graflex camera hung on a special harness on his back and he was further encumbered by a tripod and some eighteen camera sheaths loaded with 8 x 10 inch size glass plates.[23]

Nevertheless, the motorcycle gave Oliver good service for several years. On it he crisscrossed the province from Edmonton to the Montana border, over prairie, parkland and foothills and even penetrated mountain ranges. On these trips he came to know the country in a very special way, respecting its moods and glorying in its beauty. He experienced the bitterness of the north wind and the sudden warmth of a true Chinook; the fierceness of a summer thunder storm thrilled him and he responded to the heart lifting loveliness of sparkling evening sunlight on a rain drenched world. And the Rockies, close, startlingly clear in their grandeur, or remote, cloaking the secrets of their vastness, but ever beckoning—they, he must explore, their beauty, he must record.

During these years it was not the *Albertan* alone that prompted Bill Oliver's travelling. His career had expanded through an opportunity which had come his way, probably in the spring of 1912. John Cairns, editor of the *Calgary Herald*, evidently recognizing his ability as a photographer and as a newspaper man, made him an offer. Would he join the *Herald* as staff photographer? He would do his own developing and printing, and remuneration would be on a picture basis. The *Albertan* editor, strongly advised him to accept. This he did. His first pictures for the *Herald* were views of British manufacturers and civic officials at the Country Club in Calgary, which appeared on the front page on 29 June 1912.[24] Undoubtedly this was a proud day for Bill. In slightly more than two years after his arrival in a new country, he had become the first staff photographer of the city's largest newspaper.

BUILDING A CAREER

With the commencement of his work with the *Herald*, Bill Oliver's status as a photographer was assured. As the newspaper's representative he covered special events and occurrences in the city, photographed celebrities and when possible travelled into the country. With his predilection for the outdoors his main interest at this time lay in sports photography but he was always watching for anything that might be considered newsworthy.

The most important happening in Calgary during the fall of 1912 was the Stampede. It was an exciting time to be in the exuberant little city and to be involved in its activities, particularly such a unique event as its first Stampede. W.J. and his camera were busy. He photographed the Duke and Duchess of Cornwall and York; he snapped views of Indians proudly arrayed in full regalia, and took pictures of the parade.[25] An American, Milward Marcell, was designated official Stampede photographer and had exclusive coverage of the bucking and other events.

On 12 January 1913, came Bill Oliver's first major test as a news photographer. At about 12:30 on that bitterly cold Sunday morning, a night watchman at P. Burns and Company discovered fire in a storage room at the packing plant. The firm's own fire brigade was shortly joined by the city's whole fire fighting force. The men were hampered by intense cold, temperatures from 30 to 40 degrees below zero, Fahrenheit, which froze the pumps, reduced pressure from the hydrants and generally resulted in an inadequate water supply. The spray from the firemen's hoses froze instantly on their clothing, encasing them in ice and causing several cases of severe frost-bite. The men were unable to control the blaze which raged all day Sunday and on into the night, virtually the entire packing plant was destroyed.

Bill arrived on the scene in plenty of time to scoop the event for his paper. He also learned that taking pictures in such weather is difficult and hazardous; that day brought his first experience with frost-bite. Nevertheless, he captured views of many phases of the halocaust and some of his photographs of ice-laden buildings were truly spectacular. The *Herald* carried two of his pictures on the front page and two more on a subsequent page, one of which—an interior view showing ice formations resembling a labyrinth of stalagmites and stalactites—was captioned "This is Not an Arctic Ice Cave."[26] There was something ironic in this twist of fate. Through the destruction of a building in which W. J. Oliver had been denied work in the business he was qualified to pursue, he had the opportunity to demonstrate his ability in another field.

As the spring of 1913 approached, excitement flared in Calgary sports circles over an event planned by boxing promoter Tommy Burns. As a result of Burns' influence, interest in the sport had been growing and when the promoter felt that a young boxing protege of his, Arthur Pelkey, had reached championship standards he arranged a bout for him with Luther McCarty of Chicago. This was to take place in Calgary on 24 May 1913. McCarty, who had befriended Bill Oliver two years previously, had gained fame as a boxer and was being hailed as the "white" heavyweight champion of the world. Calgary now saw itself as "the hub of the boxing universe."[27] Preparations were made for the bout to be held at the Manchester arena, the event was widely advertised, and sports writers from as far away as Chicago made hotel reservations.[28]

When McCarty came to Calgary for training he quickly resumed his relationship with Bill and the boxer ensured that his friend had every opportunity to take photographs. So through the training period pictures were taken almost daily and, to cover the subject thoroughly, he obtained views from the Pelky camp.

On the day of the match, Bill was there with all the privileges of the press. The arena was crowded and when the two heavyweights came into the ring the applause was tremendous. Then, almost as soon as the fight started it was over, and McCarty lay dead. The cause, the doctors said, was a dislocated neck and resultant spinal hemorrhage. The *Herald* carried two of Oliver's pictures taken immediately before the fight,[29] while the *Albertan* reprinted the photograph of McCarty which Bill had taken the previous March, proclaiming it to be the first picture of the great Luther McCarty ever published.[30] The city was saddened; this man was respected and well liked but no one felt his loss more keenly than Bill Oliver.

Through 1913 Bill Oliver's horizons continued to broaden. Ever since his arrival in Calgary, the mountains had been call-

Beginning of the McCarty-Pelkey fight in Calgary, 1913. A few minutes later, Luther McCarty, left, died in the ring.

ing to him so during that spring he made his first motorcycle trip to Banff National Park. The journey was one with a special purpose: to photograph the scenic marvels of Banff, and if possible, Lake Louise, in all their pristine beauty. At this time man had made relatively little impact on the mountain environment.

The narrow rutted trails to Banff were bumpy and steep but probably the greatest hazards lay in crossing creeks. Some were high and the fast running water obscured the bed of the ford. At times the photographer's machine hit a submerged rock and the usual result was a dunking in the cold mountain water. On reaching Canmore he reported to the Royal North-West Mounted Police post as cyclists were required to do. At a time when only horse-drawn conveyances transported tourists into Banff, the sudden appearance of a noisy motorcycle was so frightening to horses that upsets and runaways were likely to result. The cyclists were supposed to proceed only when the police determined that the way was clear.

When the photographer eventually reached Banff he put his cycle in the livery barn as was the custom before the day of garages. The Banff scenery was beautiful and rewardingly photogenic but the cameraman had his mind set on an area even more spectacular, Lake Louise. The thought of travelling forty miles on the precipitous winding road, which might more aptly be described as a pony trail, was appalling. However, W. J. Oliver was not easily discouraged so he thought of another way. Going to the CPR station he found out the times of the westbound passenger and freight trains. Choosing a period when the line would be free from rail traffic he put his machine onto the sleepers and set off for the Laggan station. The ride was exceedingly bumpy but when travelling at a speed of about thirty-five miles an hour the vibration was minimized. His Graflex camera in its special harness on his back suffered no injury but its constant bumping against his shoulders, plus the effort of lifting the cycle over rail switches, resulted in some sore and aching muscles. However, when the photographer saw the magnificence of the views around the station there was excitement and gratification in recording such aesthetic wonders on film.[31]

From that time onward he headed for the mountains as often as possible. Frequently leaving Calgary some hours before daylight, he would cycle up to the Canmore area to spend the day with his camera. On these trips it was not the grandeur of the Rockies alone that attracted him; he had discovered the thrill of taking wild animal pictures, an area of photographic art which he was to make peculiarly his own.

Much as he enjoyed these days alone in the wilds with his camera, he appreciated the companionship of friends, too. It was probably in 1913 that he developed a close friendship which added a different and important dimension to his life. He met Tony Knights, a young man from the Millarville area, south-west of Calgary. Young Knights had decided that ranch work was not for him so had come to the city where he was engaged as an apprentice to a tinsmith. He did not enjoy this type of work either; it was photography that really appealed to him and through this interest he met Bill Oliver. It was a congenial relationship. He liked to help in the studio, assisting in developing and printing pictures, then on fine weekends, they would mount Bill's motorcycle and roar off into the foothills; their destination was Knights' home at Millarville. From the beginning the family extended a warm welcome to Tony's friend; Mrs. Knights treated him like one of her own sons and the younger children regarded him as another brother. To Bill, far away from his own family, this warm acceptance filled a gap in his life and he easily fitted in to the routine on the Knights' farm. The younger members of the family wanted rides on his motorcycle so he would take them bumping and sputtering across the fields and into the pasture to round up the milk cows. On the appearance of such a noisy apparition, the cows, instead of proceeding at a sedate pace or, more characteristically, spreading out and stopping to graze by turns, rushed for home at a most unseemingly rate. This annoyed the children's father—milk production from cows that run or get upset is noticeably reduced.[32]

As the years passed, Bill continued to spend weekends frequently with the Knights family. Besides his enjoyment of the visits, the Millarville countryside had a magnetic attraction for him. On one occasion he attempted the trip when the roads were so bad that the wheels of his Indian cycle became completely clogged with mud. At that time part of the rutted trail leading from Calgary into the foothills country to the south-west led across the Sarcee Indian Reserve. Bill traversed that

Rocky Mountain view, west of Banff

Street corner in Calgary during the 1914 oil boom

section and managed to reach the little hamlet of Priddis where he spent the night in the stopping house. The weather had improved by morning and he was anxious to make an early start. He needed something to clean the mud off his motorcycle but no one was stirring around the stopping house so he took a sheet from his bed and with that was able to remove enough of the gumbo to get his machine in running order again. Without further trouble he reached the Knights home where he spent the usual happy weekend. However, the sheet he had "borrowed" was on his mind so as soon as possible after his return to Calgary he bought a new sheet and mailed it to the keeper of the Priddis stopping house with his thanks.[33]

During Calgary's boom period each year made its own impact and brought its own special assignments for W. J. Oliver, assignments in increasing numbers as time passed. The year 1914 was one of particular moment. It marked the beginning of Calgary's love affair with oil. After the first Turner Valley well, Dingman No. 1, blew in on 14 May 1914, the city was engulfed in a wave of excitement.[34] W.J. went out to photograph the well, making the first of many camera forays into the fields. Some of his Dingman Well photographs were to become classics in the pictorial record of the Turner Valley fields.

Soon the excitement of the oil bonanza was dimmed by news of a devastating mine disaster in the Crowsnest Pass area. On 19 June 1914, the Hillcrest Collieries mine was rocked by the most terrible explosion to mar the history of Canadian mining. Located in the valley between Turtle and Hillcrest Mountains the mine, or rather two mines, penetrated the slopes of Hillcrest Mountain with a labyrinth of connecting runways and tunnels. On that morning a spark, a flaring lamp or some other unidentified cause triggered a terrific coal dust explosion, then came another. The morning shift of miners were at work in the tunnels when the blasts rained death upon them.

Word of the catalysm was telegraphed across the country. The *Calgary Herald* and other newspapers sent reporters and photographers to the scene. When Bill and the other newsmen arrived they found a valley of horror and grief. Rescue parties were bringing out shattered bodies of miners and the Royal North-West Mounted Police had assumed the grisly task of assembling the dead. They had no wish to have photographers adding to the confusion so they gave the order that no pictures of the disaster scene were to be taken.

It was a cold miserable day. A heavy mist had rolled up the valley and a chilling wind brought gusts of rain laced with stinging particles of snow.[35] The cameramen, frustrated by the "no picture" order and depressed by the tragedy, tramped back and forth in the mud cursing the whole situation. Shortly W.J. left the grumbling group; he found purposeless inactivity hard to tolerate, furthermore, when he was sent to take pictures he was determined to get them. Going to one of the policemen he handed in his Graflex camera then went into the town of Hillcrest where he bought a folding Brownie. Returning to the pithead with the little camera concealed under his oilskin raincoat, he wandered around in an innocent fashion, surreptiously snapping pictures. Then he picked up his Graflex from the police and returned to Calgary with the Hillcrest story on film. Later, he met the policeman to whom he had given his Graflex and explained what had happened regarding the mystery of the Hillcrest mine explosion pictures. He needed to use all his charm to smooth things over with the chagrined arm of the law.[36]

Then on 4 August came the frightening news of the outbreak of war. Calgary responded with enthusiastic patriotism; men hurried to join up to defend the Empire and the cause of freedom. The Calgary contingent of the Princess Patricia's Own Light Infantry boarded the train for the east on 14 August, just ten days later. They were, the *Herald* boasted, the first men from western Canada to leave for the front.[37]

Among the many young men in the Calgary area who responded quickly to the call to arms were Tony Knights and his older brother, Charlie. Both were killed in action. It was in the spring of 1915 when Tony's parents received the news of his death. Bill Oliver, too, volunteered for the army, but, surprisingly for an active young man, was placed in third category for medical reasons. His problem was varicose veins in his legs, a condition which never curtailed his outdoor activities. He was in the army for a time and was in training at Sarcee but was not accepted for active service. Meanwhile, he carried on with his photographic work. There were views to take of the Sarcee military camp and activities there, also group photographs and

View of the Turner Valley oilfield, with the Okalta well in the foreground

pictures of soldiers entraining for departure to the east and overseas.

While he was at Sarcee, Bill made another contact which had important consequences for him. He became friends with Eber Foley, a recruit who was also in the army's third category, his problem being a lung weakness causing susceptibility to pneumonia. The two men became good companions, frequently spending leisure time together. Eber worked in a sporting goods store owned by his uncle, Alex Martin, and on occasion took Bill with him to visit the Martin home. Alex Martin, a Scottish emigrant to Manitoba in 1864, had pursued many different types of work before arriving with a young family in the Calgary area in 1894. Here he worked as foreman for Lady Adela and Tom Cochrane who had founded the town of Mitford and operated a nearby sawmill; later he homesteaded briefly, then established, with his wife's brother, the Foley-Martin general store in the town of Cochrane, and in 1906 settled down with his sporting goods business in Calgary.

The mother, Alice Foley Martin, had died in 1916 and most of the older members were on their own by this time. The youngest ones, two boys, Ross and Bob, were still children and the main responsibility for their upbringing and for the operation of the household was shouldered by one of the daughters, Marjorie. The Martin home usually seemed to be thronging with young people; besides family members coming and going, there were visiting friends, many of them in the military. Bill enjoyed these occasions immensely; most particularly, he found his hostess, Marjorie Martin, completely charming. She was a young woman of twenty-three, attractive, with dark hair and eyes, a quiet efficient manner and a certain captivating air of graciousness. Soon Oliver was calling at Martin's with a regularity that bespoke his special interest.

During the deepening romantic involvement in his life, Bill Oliver continued to expand his photographic enterprises. His studio business had increased as years passed. One of his earliest clients had been Young and Kennedy Ltd., wholesale and retail stationery and office furnishers, a firm which also acted as agents for typewriters and gramophones. While carrying out a commission at this establishment one day Bill met Norman S. Rankin of the Department of Natural Resources of the CPR, a chance meeting which led to another facet of the photographer's varied career. Rankin, impressed by the young man's capability, asked if he could take time from his newspaper and other work to undertake an assignment for the CPR. Bill could always make time for interesting commissions and he thoroughly enjoyed going on photographic trips. He accompanied Rankin to Bassano and took several pictures of the irrigation dam then being constructed.[38] This was the first of many assignments completed for the railway.

An important part of the company's promotional program was the presentation of the beauty of its mountain section, and this was the type of photography in which Bill Oliver specialized. He could portray the inherent grandeur and majesty of the mountains and used light, shadows, reflections, and cloud patterns with subtle skill and artistry. Also, through infinite patience and a knowledge of the habits of animals, he was often able to catch wildlife in the perfection of its natural setting. Many of his photographs soon graced Canadian Pacific hotels and stations across the nation.[39]

As early as 1913 W. J. Oliver's studio work had grown sufficiently to warrant a move to a better situation, 214 Bruner Block, located at 1216-1 Street West. After approximately two years here he relocated at still improved premises in the Edge Block at 1211-1 Street West, where his business flourished during the late teens. However, throughout these years press photography remained the backbone of his operation.

One particularly exciting assignment was undertaken in February 1918. Paul Welch of the McLaughlin Motor Car sales department, Calgary, was planning to drive an E45 60-horsepower McLaughlin touring car to Banff. The temperature stood around fifteen degrees below zero, the road was mainly unbroken and snowfall had been heavy; also there was said to be no record of any motorized vehicle having made the trip from Calgary to Banff in other than ideal summer weather.[40] At this time many car owners prepared their motors for winter by draining radiators, removing batteries and hoisting the vehicles up on blocks to take the weight off the tires. The run would be a performance experiment for the car and, if successful, extremely good advertising for McLaughlin cars and the local dealership; in addition, it would make a fascinating news story for the *Calgary Herald*. The trip was planned to coincide with Banff's winter carnival as an added news fillip.

Bill Oliver with his movie camera

The *Herald*'s editor wanted W.J. to go on the journey and photograph the event. The party consisted of Paul Welch, Bill Oliver, and Bill Mather from the McLaughlin garage.

Braving the cold darkness of an early winter morning they left the city at 6:45 on 14 February 1918. The top of the car was up and the side curtains firmly fastened but these provided little protection from the bitter cold. After a few miles they encountered a great snow drift, the first of many. The driver's strategy was to advance the gas and tear into the drift at about fifty miles an hour. At times he would roar through; often he'd get stuck, then the three men would get busy with shovels and after a quantity of snow was dug away, Welch would take another run at the drift. It was a formidable trial for the McLaughlin and gruelling work for the men, particularly as some of the drifts, they claimed, were eight or ten feet deep.

The greatest danger came on the Anthracite hill some four miles east of Banff where the car narrowly missed sliding over a steep precipice into a canyon several hundreds of feet below. Welch was able to back the vehicle cautiously away from the brink, but to avoid travel on a dangerous ledge more hours of digging and ploughing through heavy drifts were required. Eventually they made it and the McLaughlin puffed into Banff at fifteen minutes after eight that evening. An interested crowd gathered around to hear the story of the record trip and admire the marvel of an automobile powerful enough to accomplish such a feat. The journey of eighty-two miles had taken thirteen and one half hours and used thirteen gallons of gasoline; coal oil used in the radiator worked satisfactorily, not boiling over or having to be replenished.[41]

Two days were spent at the carnival and then Welch and party headed for home, leaving Banff at half past seven in the morning of 17 February. The return journey over a broken trail was less difficult despite a sudden blizzard and new drifts on the formidable hill on the east side of the town of Cochrane. After six hours and fifty minutes of travel the McLaughlin rolled into the city; it had consumed a mere four and one half gallons of gasoline coming home, a record which its owners felt was most commendable. Indeed, the car had truly proved its ability on the trip; Oliver's pictures recorded the achievement. The *Herald*'s account of the story was illustrated by a view of the car half submerged in a great bank of snow and a later one showing it standing proudly on the main street in Banff.[42]

There were discomforts and dangers in this cameraman's career which Bill Oliver was building for himself, but it was an exciting and fascinating life and he enjoyed it.

III. Outdoor Photographer

Early in his career, Bill Oliver realized that outdoor photography was his forte. He had retained his interest in cattle and horses and was conscious of the agricultural scene and its pictorial possibilities. The *Herald*, which on its inception had appeared under the name *Calgary Herald - Mining and Ranche Advocate and Advertiser*, had remained an organ which served the ranch community of southern Alberta; over the years its mandate had expanded to include farming, irrigation, and other facets of agriculture. Therefore, the photographer and his employer shared the common goal of reflecting rural life, in addition to regular coverage of the city view and its special events and concerns.

So Bill kept a keen eye on stockmen's activities and when he heard that George Lane of the Bar U Ranch was bringing in a bunch of Percherons to ship to France for the army, he sensed a possible news story. He asked Lane if he could photograph the event; the rugged, broad-shouldered rancher stared down at him and then replied flatly, "The taking of animal pictures is an art. I don't want any pictures that make my horses look like kangaroos. . . ."[1] He relented at Bill's promise to submit prints to him for approval before publication and gave the necessary permission. The photos were good, showing the horses to be the fine animals they were, which naturally pleased the owner. It was typical of the rancher that he commended Bill Oliver for his work and recommended him to others in the ranching fraternity.

There was, however, one occasion when Lane was not at all pleased with the cameraman. He had invited him down to the Bar U Ranch to photograph his beef herd as he was preparing to ship a whole train load to Chicago; the pictures would be good advertising for the high quality of beef he raised. Bill was delighted to go. After arrival at the ranch he loaded his photographic equipment onto a saddle horse and rode out with the big boss. Finding the animals were to be driven up a gully, he located a convenient site and set up his tripod and camera complete with black focussing cloth. As the herd was steadily approaching, Bill realized he could get better pictures from another knoll a little closer to the route the steers were taking. Quickly he picked up his equipment and with the black cloth flapping, he ran towards the other knoll. To the steers, such a spectacle seemed to be like a demon from the nether world and they stampeded in every direction. The young photographer had innocently committed a cardinal sin of the range country: he had not known that cattle were likely to stampede at the sight of a man on foot, and he had doubly compounded the felony by running and carrying a fluttering object. The cowboys finally got the herd rounded up and corralled. Bill, circumspectly this time, took his pictures, and George Lane was so pleased with them that he overlooked the stampede incident.

Some time later, through a chance occurrence, Bill Oliver demonstrated abilities which surprised and impressed the veteran stockman. He was asked to photograph a round-up on Emerson's Flats. The wagons rolled out one evening and the next morning W.J. and the boss set out with a team and buckboard. After a few miles drive they discovered a steer with a broken leg. Lane, following the practice of stockmen in dealing with such range cattle tragedies, pulled out his rifle and shot the animal to end its suffering. It was a healthy two-year old and he mentioned that he wished he had a knife so he could bleed the carcass and have the beef for the ranch consumption. Bill produced his knife and, much to the rancher's amusement, offered to do the job—it was hardly an undertaking for a city-based photographer with no ranch experience. However, Bill got busy and, to his companion's surprise, he deftly bled, skinned, and dressed the beef in a professional manner. Lane had a new respect for the young man. As a further test he asked the photographer to help select good steers for shipment and to estimate their weights. Again Bill's performance impressed the stockman and as a man who knew something about cattle he rose considerably in the rancher's estimation. As a result, Lane's commissions and his outspoken commendation helped give Bill Oliver the status of official photographer for most of the leading ranchers of southern Alberta.

Another well known rancher who gave Bill a number of commissions was A. E. Cross, founder of the Calgary Brewing

Branding at the Bar U Ranch, ca.1919

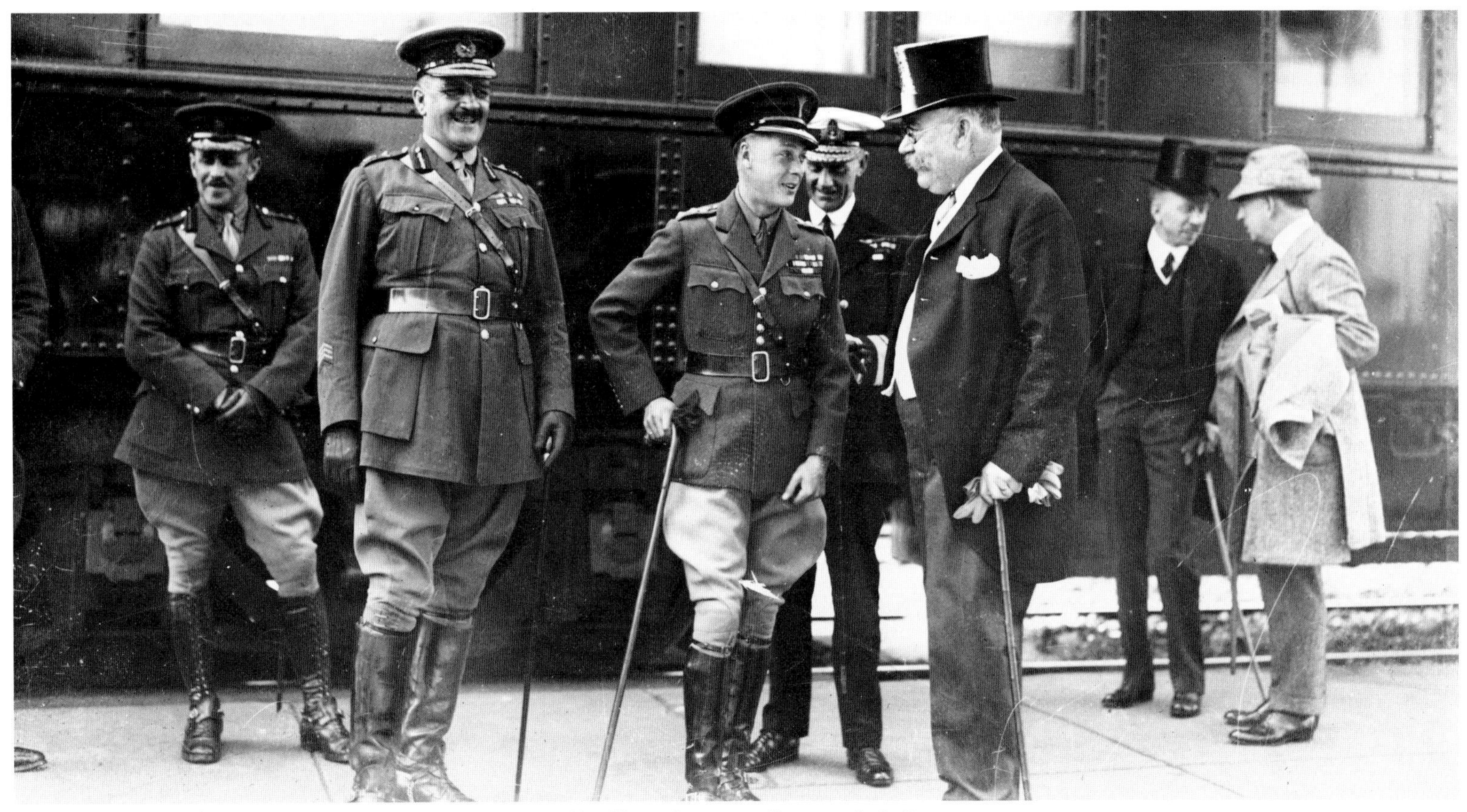

Edward, Prince of Wales, arriving in Calgary, 1919. He was greeted by Alberta Lieutenant-Governor R. G. Brett.

and Malting Company and a noted Alberta cattle man. On one occasion W.J. was asked to photograph a round-up of Cross's A7 Ranch cattle in the Lundbreck area. He set out riding with Jim, the owner's son, and obtained some excellent views of the herd on the flats against the magnificent backdrop of the mountains. The cattle were to ford the Oldman River north of Lundbreck so, deciding to photograph the action, Bill crossed to the far side and found an appropriate place partly concealed by some bushes. The cattle were headed in that direction, then an old cow spotted the intruder and charged towards him on the run, the rest of the herd pounding after her. Suddenly the old cow swerved, the herd split and the cattle passed on either side of him. When Jim Cross galloped up, fearful of what he might find, W.J. and his gear were unharmed. The photographer didn't seem too concerned but later he admitted that it "had been a nervous time."[2]

Occurrences similar to this were not altogether unusual for the official ranch photographer in the late teens and twenties. It was exciting but there was also more mundane work to be done around the city. Calgary at this time was going through a transition period. With the end of the war, the business of converting to peacetime living commenced, a change that could not be effected quickly. There were problems related to the re-establishment of the soldiers who returned and to the disastrous flu epidemic of the period. During the same time the city enjoyed some happy events, including the 1919 visit of His Royal Highness, Edward, Prince of Wales.

The city planned a special welcome with a series of festive functions, the main events being a public reception at the Exhibition Grounds, a garden party at the Sir James Lougheed home, a luncheon at the Palliser Hotel, and a military ball. The prince was charming in a boyish natural way and the city enthusiastically took him to its collective heart. His third day in Alberta was to be spent privately and comparatively restfully at George Lane's Bar U Ranch.

A number of privileged press writers and photographers representing newspapers from across the country were travelling with the royal party but they were encountering a serious problem with His Royal Highness' official photographer. This man, possibly uncertain regarding his own position in the prince's retinue, asserted the authority of his position and in the eyes of the Canadian photographers became downright officious. The understanding had been that he would be responsible for all photography of a private nature for the prince while the other cameramen would shoot news photos of him at public functions. In actual practice the local photographers were relegated to the background and the official photographer's pictures were the ones appearing in Canadian newspapers. The photographers' grievances were further aggravated by the news that no Canadian cameramen were to accompany the party to the Bar U.

W. J. Oliver as staff photographer of the host city's largest newspaper, had had no problem in obtaining good pictures of the prince at the station, with war veterans, on platforms, inspecting cadets and at various other functions, including an excellent close view of His Highness waving from the train.[3] Now W.J. had every intention of joining the royal entourage at the ranch. Fortunately, he had been commissioned by George Lane several weeks earlier to take a series of pictures at the ranch during the prince's visit. The other press men wished him luck and waited, probably not too hopefully, for results. Another photographer, who thought that if he were on the scene he might manage to get a picture asked Oliver to give him a lift. Bill had been asked by George Lane to take out some extra luggage so shortly after the royal party left High River, he, too, started for the Bar U with the luggage placed in the back and the determined Canadian beside him. After travelling a few miles Bill realized that some of the vehicles in front had stopped and apparently were waiting for him. At that point, his companion ducked down onto the floorboards and Bill threw a rug over him. All photographic equipment was also tucked out of sight. On being challenged concerning his right to be following the royal cavalcade, Bill explained innocently and truthfully that he was conveying baggage to the ranch. Pieces of luggage were in plain sight in the back of his car and the English security official allowed him to proceed. They reached the ranch without further incident.

Early next morning W. J. Oliver and his camera were on hand waiting for the prince to emerge from the ranch house. The official photographer appeared first and his wrathful objections to a local photographer on the scene were promptly overridden when George Lane explained that this young man was *his* official photographer and there at his express request. The big rancher was forceful and accustomed to being obeyed; besides this was his property and the prince and entourage

Edward, Prince of Wales, with George Lane, right, on the Bar U Ranch, 1919

were his guests. There was nothing more to be said and the Englishman accepted the situation with good grace. However, when the stowaway photographer appeared with his camera he was ordered to return his equipment to the bunkhouse immediately and to leave it there or he would not be allowed to continue with the party on the remainder of the itinerary.

The prince was truly interested in the ranch and its activities. A round-up was in progress and the heir to the British throne insisted on helping the cowboys. He inspected a band of Percheron mares to be shipped to England and participated in a little grouse or duck shooting expedition. Bill Oliver photographed him in these unusual pursuits and then obtained his permission to take some more intimate and extremely appealing pictures.[4] At the end of the day Bill phoned his colleagues in Calgary, picked up his erstwhile travelling companion who had been banished to the bunkhouse and rushed off to Calgary. His studio that night was a crowded busy place; the Canadian press photographers were there to assist so the negatives were developed and prints made with all possible speed. By midnight photographs of the prince on the Bar U were in the mail addressed to papers across Canada, to England, and every part of the British Empire. It was indeed a triumph for Bill Oliver. He rode his wave of success still farther the next day when he shot more pictures of the prince in Banff being made "Chief Morning Star" of the Stoney Indians.

Shortly after this, Lane called Bill back to the ranch to make a thorough photographic survey of the Beddingfeld ranch immediately west of the Bar U. Afterwards he learned that these pictures were submitted to King George V when his approval was being sought for the purchase of this ranch. Just a month after the royal visit the news came that the prince had bought the Beddingfeld Ranch.

Another happy event which Calgary experienced in 1919 was the Victory Stampede. The first Stampede in 1912 had been a smashing success, but then a war had come and now the world, attitudes, everything, had changed. Would the people respond again to a Stampede? The city wanted to have some mammoth type of entertainment to celebrate the return of the soldiers from overseas and Calgarians were never adverse to taking a chance, so the Victory Stampede was held.

Cowboys and some cowgirls from across the continent were there, competition was keen, and events were most successful. Surprisingly, however, the city did not seem to enter into the festival in its customary wholehearted way. Attendance was not as good as expected. The *Herald* gave the Stampede complimentary write-ups but not front page treatment. The main stories dealt with the pageantry and excitement of the prince's arrival in eastern Canada and his triumphant progress there. At this time, too, the automobile was coming into its own and the *Herald* gave coverage to calls for better roads, the joys of motoring, the scenic wonders of the Circle Tour which followed a route from Calgary to Banff, down the Windermere, then east through the Crowsnest, past Pincher Creek, to Fort Macleod and back to Calgary. The latter article was illustrated by a number of Oliver photographs.[5] Possibly the timing of the Victory Stampede had not been the best.

As staff photographer for the *Herald*, W. J. Oliver had a pass which gave him access not only to the Stampede grounds but to behind the scenes areas. By this time, he had become skillful in catching the action of wildly plunging horses, twisting Brahma steers, and fast moving cowboys. One of his pictures in 1919—a view of noted Alberta rider Clem Gardner on a horse called High Tower—was claimed to be the model for cowboy artist Edward Borein's famous Stampede picture "I-See-You." It shows the horse practically standing on its hind legs with its head slightly twisted sideways as though to eye the man still seated in easy control in the saddle.[6]

Bill learned that to take these exciting action pictures he had to be dangerously close to the contestants. As a rodeo photographer he entered the infield itself and at times to his peril found himself participating in the action. He had to be quick thinking and fast moving. Split second decisions in taking a picture, anticipating a bronc's next move, and avoiding pounding hooves were required. Being a good sprinter was also a valuable asset. For photographing bucking horses Bill used a special method, probably an original one, to assess his danger. If the horse came out of the chute with eyes open, Bill moved in to try for a picture, but if the bronc bucked blind, the photographer made for the nearest fence. Such a horse was, he contended, particularly dangerous; indeed one knocked him flying and completely smashed his camera. On another occasion he

Clem Gardner on *High Tower* at the Calgary Stampede, 1919. This photograph was the inspiration for artist Edward Borien's work, "I-See-You."

was absorbed in photographing a cowboy who was wrestling a steer to the ground. However, an animal released by the previous contestant was still at large and, suddenly seeing a man on foot, charged at Oliver's unsuspecting back. When the crowd yelled a warning, the photographer glanced behind him, clutched his camera, and ran for the fence, the steer hard on his heels. He grabbed the top strand on the six-foot fence and started pulling himself up, when suddenly he was boosted from behind. The impetus from the thrust of the steer's head sent him sailing over the fence with feet to spare. The crowd roared its appreciation. Bill's first thought, as always, was for the safety of his camera but it had come through the ordeal unscathed and he had suffered nothing worse than a few bruises.[7]

Later, after his assistant, Walter Cadman, received a more serious toss over the fence, Stampede officials decided that the cameramen needed some protection so they made a photographers' pit and erected a fence in front of it. This was infinitely safer, although occasionally plunging hooves sent the fence flying.[8]

The spring of 1920 marked the end of Bill Oliver's first decade in Canada. He had come a long way since he arrived in Calgary in 1910, alone and friendless. Now, no longer a green Englishman, he was attune to the western Canadian mood. He had been a part of Calgary and area during those formative years. He also had lost his English accent, possibly in reaction to the anti-English sentiment he had encountered during his first weeks in Calgary, or perhaps it was a natural outcome of his Canadianization process. Always having an affinity with the country, he had come to feel himself truly Canadian. Now when he walked down Calgary's streets he was hailed by many people from all walks of life who greeted a fellow Albertan with warmth and respect. He had developed warm friendships with his colleagues on the *Herald* and many others with whom he came in contact.

It was typical of the photographer's wholehearted approach to life that he participated in community affairs. When plans were under way for forming the downtown Kiwanis Club in 1919, he was one of the seventy-five charter members. He was a Mason and joined the Alberta Royal Arch Masons. The Shriners, too, attracted his attention and he became an active

Niler Foser being pitched off a Brahma steer at the Calgary Stampede

Beginning of the wild cow milking contest, Calgary Stampede, 1934

member of the Al Azhar Temple. These fraternal contacts and the social life in which he became involved were important to him, although perhaps his most poignant moments came when the city was far behind and the countryside brought to him its peace and the balm of its beauty.

Without doubt Bill Oliver's social life and his leisure hours had acquired a new meaning during the years since he had met Marjorie Martin. He spent as much time as he could in her company and they found they had much in common. Partly, perhaps, as a legacy of her childhood spent in the Cochrane area, Marjorie had an interest in horses and liked to ride; indeed, she, too, had an appreciation of outdoor activities so enjoyed accompanying him on hikes and drives into the country. Bill had graduated from motorcycles to automobiles and by 1917 he was driving a McLaughlin Buick. The Banff Winter Carnival attracted them and during summers there were fishing expeditions and short trips into the country, these on occasion being combined with photographing assignments.

The marriage took place on 22 September 1920, and later that day they drove southward towards the Bar U Ranch and a rather unusual honeymoon. A short time before this, George Lane had asked Bill to photography his beef herd and other stock on the ranch during the last week in September. For once Bill demurred, explaining that he would be spending that week on his honeymoon. Lane had a ready solution—he and his family would be away so the photographer and his bride could have the ranch house to themselves, complete with the services of the Chinese cook. The foreman and ranch hands would be busy with their usual work but saddle horses would be available at any time. The photographic work would not be onerous and they would in effect have the Bar U at their disposal for a week's holiday. Bill liked the idea and Marjorie agreed; probably she was already aware that she would always have to share her husband with his camera in a special sort of way. The week was idyllic. The weather was fine and the couple spent many golden hours riding over the Bar U range, splendid in the autumnal beauty of the foothills.

Bill had bought a house at 1412 Shelbourne Street, doubtless rejoicing that his days in rooming houses were over. He and Marjorie moved in shortly after their return to Calgary and this remained their home for many years.

EXPANSION ACROSS CANADA AND BEYOND

The twenties and thirties were extremely active and productive years for W. J. Oliver. His business continued to grow, expanding beyond the press work for the *Herald* and the *Albertan*, and the demands of his private studio activities. In true entrepreneur style he adopted an enterprising approach to his profession and was always discovering and trying new lines of endeavour. One of these brought him into association with the Topical Press Agency of Fleet Street, London.

Topical Press, founded in 1903, was said to have been the first business of its kind, an agency for the procurement of photographs and their distribution for publication to newspapers, magazines, and books. Such outlets paid a reproduction fee for use of a picture, seldom making an outright purchase. Photographers and photographic firms on a world-wide basis used the services of this company. Its founder and operator was Walter J. Edwards, universally known as "Toppy" Edwards, this nickname having been derived from the name of his agency. Probably W.J. first submitted pictures to Topical Press in the late teens. During the next two decades he sent a wide range of scenic and wildlife photographs to the London company, excellent pictures with regard to both clarity of detail and artistic quality.

Bill Oliver's association with this firm and its owner extended beyond that of a business relationship. From the beginning there had been a bond of mutual respect and esteem between the two men which had ripened into a strong friendship. Just when they first met is not known, but possibly it was in 1918 when Bill was in England for his father's funeral. In any event, when Edwards visited Calgary at the time of the Prince of Wales' visit in 1919, the two men were already on friendly terms.

In 1922 the two met again. At this time Bill had taken his wife and little daughter Joan to England. They spent some time with Bill's mother and brother, Reg, at the Orchard and later he took his family on a little tour which included a visit in the Toppy Edward's home. From this time onwards throughout the twenties the Olivers and the Edwards met frequently either in Canada or England.[9]

Another facet of Bill Oliver's free lance photography was his

Stooks on General Strange Flats near Namaka, east of Calgary, ca.1920s

work for the National Parks Branch. During the war years and the period immediately following, the market for photographs was restricted, nevertheless W.J. optimistically had expanded his picture taking activities, partly for personal pleasure and partly for future use. His camera trips into the mountains and adjacent foothills had resulted in the accumulation of a collection of outstanding photographs of scenery and wildlife. It was probably in 1921 that he commenced submitting these to the National Parks Branch. During that year, a publicity and information division was established by Parks Commissioner J. B. Harkin, and J. C. Campbell was appointed its director. The function of the newly-formed division was to publicize the national parks, their objectives and attractions. For this purpose a program of producing informational booklets, reprinting earlier publications and writing news and feature articles concerning the parks was instituted; in addition a library of photographs and lantern slides was organized.[10]

Again W. J. Oliver demonstrated his flair for making a move at the most propitious time. He approached the Parks Branch with photographs portraying the scenic beauties and wildlife of Banff National Park just when the branch had adopted a policy which required such material. The Annual Report of the Commissioner for Parks for 1921-1922 contains a picture which is probably among the first which W.J. provided for the Parks Branch. It is a view of a moose in shallow water, possibly at Emerald Lake, and carries a credit line, "Photo by W. J. Oliver."[11] Thus began a long, happy and mutually beneficial association. During the 1920s and 1930s, Oliver travelled widely in the national parks across Canada. Riding Mountain, Prince Albert, Cape Breton Highlands, the Pacific rim were all on his photographic route, but the bulk of his work was done in the national parks in Alberta and British Columbia. These included Waterton Lakes, Banff, Jasper, Yoho, Kootenay, Glacier, Elk Island, Buffalo Park at Wainwright, and the antelope reserve park at Nemiskam.[12] Arrangements were made for him to accompany park wardens on their routine trips. He joined their pack horse outfits, looking after his own horse and gear, and daily photographing scenic gems. Constantly on the alert for wild animals he learned much about their habits and obtained many excellent wildlife pictures.

The Parks Branch required pictorial coverage of some of the more mundane activities within its parks, also. For example, in view of the policy of encouraging the public to travel in the parks, increasing attention was paid to roads and road construction. Consequently a good proportion of Bill Oliver's photographs dealt with roads and motoring; views showing a car, usually a touring model, on a rough, narrow, often precipitous road dwarfed by the majesty of the mountains, typify mountain travel of the period. The construction in 1922 and 1923 of the Banff-Windmere highway, a gravel road some sixteen feet wide, marked an important milestone in Rocky Mountain motoring.[13] Work on the road had commenced in 1911 but had been interrupted by the war. However, adventuresome drivers had traversed the rough trail and Bill had photographed it at least as early as 1919. During its construction he made other photographing trips and when the official opening took place at Kootenay Crossing on 30 June 1923, he covered the event for the Parks Branch and his newspaper. Whether or not he produced a film of this event or the construction of the Windmere Highway is not clear but subsequently many road building projects in the parks were recorded by stills and films.

During this period W. J. Oliver was commissioned to take pictures around Banff, Jasper, Waterton, and other townsites in addition to photographing skiing, hiking, swimming, and a variety of parks' activities. And always there were scenic mountain pictures to take. These were not just views taken at random. He visualized the artistic effect he wished to obtain and would wait with infinite patience until appropriate conditions were met. For example, at times he would sit and wait for a cloud to reach a specific position or for a cloud formation to assume a certain pattern. He travelled to Jasper on three successive years until he got the pictures he wanted of Mount Robson. Hoping to catch a clear view of the peak in first morning light he would rise early and be off with his camera before daybreak; on the third try at approximately 5 a.m., the mists cleared and he got the picture he desired.[14]

Meanwhile, as Bill Oliver's business continued to grow, so did his studio requirements. By the end of the teens there were complaints about the amount of water used in the photo lab so he was requested to pay an extra charge which he did not feel was justified.[15] As a result, by 1920 the Oliver studio had been

The Iron Gates in Sinclair Canyon, near Radium, B.C., ca.1930s

relocated in the Lee-Arnold Building, 328A-8 Avenue West. This location, in the heart of the city and within a mere three blocks of the *Herald*, was a desirable one and here he was destined to remain.

In 1923 his studio staff was augmented by Walter Cadman, just out from England. A native of Sandwich, Kent, he had heard about the man from the neighbouring village of Ash who had gone to Calgary and established a successful photographic business. He called at the Calgary studio soon after his arrival and inquired about job possibilities. The city was still suffering from the recession which followed World War One and jobs were scarce but it is likely that Bill's own experiences as a green Englishman were recalled to his mind. Although Cadman, just seventeen, had never taken a picture and knew nothing of developing film, he was offered a job in the studio. He joined a staff of five, exclusive of the owner, which included two comparatively long term employees, Sid Reeves who had been with the firm for approximately eight years and Ed Young who had joined in 1919 or early 1920. In addition during that spring of 1923 the staff included three young women, two of whom were Marjorie Oliver's sister, Jessie Martin, and Jem M. McLeod, a close friend of the Martin family.[16]

All film developing and printing procedures were done by hand. In the darkroom there were three forty-eight gallon tanks, one each for the developing, washing, and fixing steps. Each tank could hold a hundred rolls of film for amateur work but ordinarily eighty rolls were processed at a time to avoid the possibility of film strips touching each other. Time clocks were set for ten-minute timing of films in the developer and fast paced teamwork was required to keep the films progressing smoothly and expertly through the various processing steps. By noon on an average day the developed negatives of some three hundred rolls of film were hanging in the drying room where the air was circulated by fans to hasten drying.

For a novice in the darkroom, perhaps the most difficult part of the procedure was the special technique required for unrolling and stripping the film, while hand numbering the negatives was the most tedious. During most afternoons prints were made and again teamwork was the keynote of the operation. At least four people were invloved from cutting up the negatives to the production of the finished print. Trays and small tanks approximately 38 × 40 inches and eight inches deep were used for the acid bath which had to be prepared by mixing various chemicals. The washing procedure which followed the hypo bath was done in a drum powered by water pressure. Next the prints were placed on black enamel ferrotype plates, 18 × 24 inches in size, and large sheets of blotting paper pressed on top. Again fans assisted drying.[17]

The studio was equipped with several enlargers. The machine which produced 5 × 7 inch prints worked automatically but the 8 × 10 enlarger required focusing. Another interesting item was a long black box appropriately referred to as "the coffin"; this was a printer used for producing circuit pictures. The box was fitted with a platen top held by springs and could print pictures up to six feet in length. Earlier, W.J. had obtained a circuit camera which he had used extensively in taking army groups as well as panoramic scenes.

The amount and variety of photographic work carried out by the studio required a battery of cameras. Foremost among these were Graphic cameras for 4 × 5 and 5 × 7 pictures and a large Graflex for taking 5 × 7s. The latter, heavy and more awkward to use, was a very dependable camera. For movie work Bill originally had an old Universal camera which required mounting on a tripod. Later he purchased a Bell & Howell Eyemo, a hand camera in which different-sized lenses could be used.[18]

For exterior pictures at this time, a photographer had to judge the setting by definition of the image as he saw it through his camera lens and by his instinctive feeling for the brightness of the light and the darkness of the object being photographed. In addition he worked with slow film, a rating of ten being usual. Orthochromatic and the slightly faster Super Speed film were the brand names of the film Bill Oliver generally used in the early 1920s. Taking flash pictures was a complicated procedure, with magnesium metal powder being used with a flash gun. The apparatus had two rubber tubes, one of which reached the top outlet, an opening consisting of two leaf-like parts enclosing an asbestos top soaked with wood alcohol. This was lighted, then the magnesium powder was blown through from the other tube producing a flash when it reached the flame. By practically continuous blowing one could retain a flash from three to five minutes. The operator had to breathe with caution; an indrawn breath with the tube still in his mouth had a distinctly unpleasant result. Various improvements in indoor picture taking followed each other in fairly quick succession. There was the explosive flash which was fired by electricity through the use of a fuse. The flash powder was set out on a tray to which the fuse was connected. A push button switch activated the device, exploding the powder with a bright light and a great volume of smoke. In fact it was necessary to use flash bags some six feet square to, hopefully, contain the smoke. Unfortunately this large object ballooning out cut down the light to some extent. From this evolved a hand flash gun operated by a spring that when released caused a spark from a flint which ignited the powder on the pan of the gun. As in all flash powder devices, expertise was required to determine the right amount of powder to use. Too little minimized the amount of light; too much caused vibration on the camera. Finally came flash bulbs, a major advancement in indoor photography and one which set the trend for future development. The Oliver Studio commenced using bulbs with reflectors about 1930.

Handling material as volatile as flash powder could be extremely dangerous as Sid Reeves of the Oliver Studio learned during the civic election day in 1922. Voting figures were posted on a large bulletin board on the back of the *Herald* Building and Reeves was sent to photograph the large crowd gathered in the evening to watch the results. Electric power for the flash gun was provided through an extension cord running out of the *Herald* Building but when Reeves pressed the switch, nothing happened. He bent over to see if something was wrong with the fuse when suddenly the flash exploded in his face—he had neglected to turn off the electric switch. His eyebrows and lashes were completely gone and much of his hair burned. He had some burns on his face but the great fear was for his eyes. However, he was fortunate as his sight was not damaged and after a short stay in hospital he was back on the job again. Thereafter he was extremely careful with flash materials.[19]

The variety which was the keynote of W. J. Oliver's career was reflected in the work carried out in his studio. There was the handling of pictures taken for the Parks Branch, for Topical Press, the CPR, the CNR, portraits and other studio commissions, and always the *Herald* assignments which covered a wide range of activities in Calgary and around much of the province. In addition there was photographic processing for various drug stores. Ten or so of the city's major drug stores, as well as a number from surrounding towns, sent the film brought in by their customers to the Oliver Studio for developing.

Periodically, there were other interesting or unusual jobs.

The W. J. Oliver Studio, Calgary, ca.1920s

For example, there was an assignment from Alberta Government Telephones to photograph telephone poles and lines around the country; again at times the Mounted Police required photographs of scenes of crimes to assist in criminal investigations. One request that appeared to be quite ordinary, that of taking a three-generations photograph, proved to be surprisingly bizarre. Bill was given to understand that the matter was urgent, that the picture should have been taken earlier, so obligingly he acted promptly. Family members were ready when he arrived at the home and obviously to both children and adults this was a serious occasion. The reason for the sober expressions became clear when he was ushered into the inner room where the photograph was to be taken. The grandfather, who had been spoken of in a manner befitting the star of the show, was stretched out on a table, clad in his best attire—but very dead. When the family arranged themselves around the head of the table, the photographer explained that the angle was wrong and that one person in a horizontal position and others vertical could not be properly arranged in a group. They tried tilting the table with no better results. Finally, they rolled an empty beer barrel into the room and the body was seated on this supported on either side by relatives. The family then grouped around the patriarch and the photograph was taken.[20]

During the 1920s, Oliver studio work was usually carried out by a staff of six or seven people in addition to Bill himself, but in busy periods, such as Stampede week, extra temporary workers were hired and as many as ten people might be employed. At times like this when the pressure for immediate newspaper pictures was great, Oliver studio staff reversed the image when printing to save the *Herald* precious minutes in the engraving process. This was a good idea but if the *Herald* engravers were not alert and reversed the image again, embarrassing pictures printed backwards would result.[21]

When W.J. was away Reeves was in charge of the studio; he left the firm and set up a business of his own in 1927. From that time on Walter Cadman took charge during the times the boss was absent. When in the city W.J. was constantly in and out of the studio as he carried out assignments in the area and despite his many trips, the activities of his business received his close attention and direction. His own work was excellent; he was never satisfied with anything less than his best effort and he expected the same careful attention and results from his staff. There was a happy atmosphere in the studio, with the permanance of staff attesting to good working relationships.

Bill Oliver on the roof of the Palliser Hotel photographing downtown Calgary, ca.1920s

IV. Movie Making

The idea of making movies had always intrigued Bill Oliver. The concept of portraying action and life, of capturing the realism and feeling of movement appealed particularly to a man of his temperment. Here was a medium which could bring a special dimension to photography and he was quick to realize its potential. At least as early as 1917 he owned a movie camera and during the late teens he spent time experimenting with it and learning the techniques of motion picture production.

Probably the most ambitious of Bill's early films was one of the Waterton Lake area. This was taken on his 1919 camping trip; a series of still photographs also recorded the outing. This perhaps fostered a special feeling for the beauties of Waterton and its film possibilities; at later dates he made further films in this park. Another significant movie was made in 1921. The film and accompanying stills were commissioned by the Matador Ranch Company which was closing out its operation at Swift Current, Saskatchewan, and moving the Canadian stock to Dakota. There was a herd of 6,000 head of cattle to trail south and it was decided to swim the animals across the South Saskatchewan River. Bill found the whole project fascinating. First there was an old time roundup with three chuckwagons and some twenty-five cowboys. The river was high and the men knew they had a difficult time ahead of them. The cattle were gathered and held in herds near the ranch headquarters. They were kept corralled and without water for twenty-four hours, and during the night two bulls were ferried across the river and staked out on the opposite bank. The bulls acted as decoys; by early morning their bellowing was echoing across the water and the cattle in the corral were milling and excited. Enticed by the bawling and goaded by their own thirst they made a wild rush for the river as soon as the corral gates were opened. The cowboys were ready—stripped to the waist they rode and yelled on the flanks and at the rear of the herd trying to force the animals to swim across. It was a good start but the work of getting the great herd across took two weeks.[1] Meanwhile, Bill was grinding away with his cameras. One of his stills, a view of a large bunch of the Matador Herefords starting into the river, was used later as a cover photograph on the *Canadian Cattlemen* magazine.[2]

During the middle 1920s W. J. Oliver's film-making ambitions received a special impetus through his appointment in 1924, or possibly earlier, as a Canadian representative of Fox News of New York. At that time, Fox News had arrangements with approximately ten Canadian cameramen to submit short slips of newsworthy subjects. The best of these each week were used in the news stories which preceded the main features in movie theatres across the country. Initially W.J. represented Alberta but later his commission was extended to include the region west of the Great Lakes across the prairie provinces and into British Columbia.

During the years 1925 to 1929, when the Fox program was terminated, W. J. Oliver was awarded a bonus for the "Best Enterprise" seven times, the "Best Photography" bonus twenty-four times, and on one occasion a special photographic bonus for a film portraying glaciers in the Rockies.[3] In addition, he twice won the annual prize for the operator whose work had given the most satisfaction during the year.[4] Winners were determined by the awarding of points throughout the year. As might be expected only a portion of the footage covering a certain subject was actually used in a news film, usually just enough to provide the framework of the story. The film might be reduced to eighty feet or less, while the use of a reel of 200 to 250 feet was unusual. Payment was made for film footage used—in 1925 the rate was $1.00 per foot. The bonuses were normally $5.00 each although sometimes $25 was paid, and the annual award in 1925 was $1,000.[5] These amounts were substantial at a period when a man's business suit with extra trousers could be bought for $30 to $35; a ladies' silk dress for $10; pure wool blankets from Scotland $8.95; a bottle of Lethbridge pure malt ale 35 cents; a performance at the Grand Theatre, Calgary, 35 or 50 cents for the best seats; and a Ford car for $617.

So Bill found the provision of news footage for Fox News worthwhile financially and in addition there was the challenge involved in finding unique or unusual subjects and in producing good work. One of his early submissions which gained him "The Best Enterprise" award and complimentary comments in the Fox bulletin in 1925 was indeed unusual. He had heard that the wife of a Calgary doctor was accustomed to exercise in her backyard every day regardless of weather. She agreed to cooperate so Bill obtained a film of her, clad as was her custom in a bathing suit, performing her exercises against a background of snowdrifts and glistening snow laden evergreens in St. George's Island park. Another unique contribution which the Fox editor, George H. K. Mitford, claimed was the best of its kind he had ever seen, pictured an Alberta turkey farm. It, too, earned an enterprise bonus. Possibly W.J.'s most noteworthy Fox News film was an aerial one. In October, 1925, he made a photographing plane journey from High River down the mountain chain and over Waterton Park. The film was claimed to be the first aerial moving picture taken of Waterton and in that part of the mountains.[6] It was a flight in which the frail aircraft penetrated the vastness of the mountains, circling steeply to miss ridges, and catching the beauty of their might and rugged splendour in a new perspective. The film was so spectacular that Mitford decided to give it the entire space available for Canadian subjects in the newsreel that week. Fox News headquarters in New York then wrote requesting all of the original footage and their edited version was shown across America and in all foreign editions of Fox News for several weeks.[7]

In May 1925, Bill Oliver learned that Captain Albert Carter, a flyer with the High River air station, had made a parachute jump from the remarkable height of 1,200 feet, so he quickly packed his cameras and took the south bound train. Before reaching High River he had devised an unusual photographic plan and with his customary enthusiastic approach he had no difficulty in selling it to the parachute jumper and his pilot, "Punch" Dickens. The three of them soon were ascending in the small plane for a repeat performance. At the right moment Captain Carter jumped out to start his descent, but this time Oliver's small movie camera was strapped above his knee and as Carter pressed the button it photographed the receding plane, the opening of the parachute, the whirling landscape far below, then coming closer and closer. Meanwhile as the plane circled the parachutist, Bill leaned out and took pictures of his descent. By the time Capt. Carter reached the ground some seventeen minutes after leaving the plane, the photographer was there recording his landing.[8] Such news films had particular appeal to audiences of the period because of the widespread interest in flying. Bill Oliver had a particular interest in aerial photography. He flew with most of the bush pilots of the

Bill Oliver, working on fishing film, 1920s

Part of the Matador Ranch herd preparing to cross the South Saskatchewan River, 1921

day—"Wop" May, "Punch" Dickens, Freddie McCall, Jock Palmer, and shared the thrill of flight with them in a small plane.

In 1923 the Canada Air Board selected the High River aerodome as a stop on the transcontinental air route; it was used also as the province's major forestry patrol station.[9] A year later, five new machines, Navro-Vipers with 200 hp. Viper engines, were acquired for the High River Station and six pilots were employed, some for forest fire patrol flying and some for photo survey work.[10] Bill Oliver frequently accompanied the pilots on their forestry patrol work. If there weren't telltale spirals of smoke to photograph, always there was magnificent mountain scenery. High River, too, was a base for geological survey flights over the foothills area, centring on Turner Valley. Ted Link, a noted geologist with Imperial Oil, was particularly interested in this work and often hired Bill Oliver to take series of aerial survey photographs. These low altitude pictures revealed anticline rock structure and specific characteristics of the terrain providing data helpful to Link and other geologists in locating oilwell drilling sites.[11]

There were opportunities, too, for aerial photography over Alberta's cities and down its main transportation corridors which Bill was quick to grasp. He was reputed to be the first man to take aerial pictures over Calgary,[12] and his aerial view of "the heart of the city"[13] taken in May, 1929, gained special prominence. For this picture, he flew over Calgary in a DeHaviland Moth biplane with Capt. Fred McCall at the controls. As the plane made a low altitude sweep over the *Herald* Building at a speed of a hundred miles per hour, he leaned from the cockpit to snap the view. The *Herald* used this particular view for a full-page illustrated explanation of the process through which a picture went before appearing in the paper. The article entitled, "A Plane Picture's Progress into Print" included twelve accompanying photographs beginning with Bill leaning from the plane to shoot the scene he saw below. There was a view of the negative being developed at the Oliver Studio, several showing the print's progression at the engravers, and a series illustrating the final steps as the front page of the paper took shape.[14]

A year later, a National Air Tour was held in Calgary. Bill Oliver joined the group in Edmonton and flew south in the DeForest-Crosley radio plane photographing competing air ships en route. Meanwhile, Walter Cadman, a passenger in a Stinson-Detroiter, took pictures of the planes as they approached the city. The films were dropped off in specially-constructed little parachutes, then rushed to the Oliver Studio to be processed for fast publication.[15] Following demonstrations of formation flying and aerial acrobatics during the afternoon came the climax of the event. This was the turning on of a huge beacon which had been erected as an aid to pilots. The beam signalled the start of a brilliant aerial display—planes flung out fireworks and trailed brilliantly coloured lights as they dipped and soared. Through radio and loudspeakers the thousands of watchers followed the steps of the performance.[16]

Another aerial event which Bill Oliver photographed occurred after Trans-Canada Air Lines had taken over continental mail service in 1938. The following year branch lines in Alberta were established and the commencement of this service presented an occasion worthy of recording.[17] On 20 August 1939, Bill Oliver and Walter Cadman, passengers in a small plane operated by Ted Holmes, a pilot with Anglo-Canadian Oils, followed the mail plane. As it flew from Calgary to Medicine Hat, to Lethbridge, back to Calgary, and then to Edmonton they filmed its progress. At one point when Bill, camera to eye, was filming from the door, the plane lurched in a down draft, forcefully jolting the camera and giving the photographer a black eye. This was one of the hazards of airborne photography before the use of aerial cameras. When Holmes and his passengers landed at the airport in Calgary later that afternoon they were met by the Mounted Police. With the world on the verge of war, the authorities wanted to know why a small aircraft was following, circling, and photographing a mail plane. It was not difficult for the cameramen to prove that the purpose of the trip was the making of a movie for the Canadian National Railway.[18]

Among the most exciting features of the Canadian scene during the 1920s, and indeed earlier, were the silk trains. These carried raw silk, actually live silk worms in their cocoons carefully packed and tied in bales, on the last lap of their journey to markets, usually in New York. The bales were rushed by fast Canadian Pacific steamships, Empress vessels, from the Orient to Vancouver where with all possible haste they were transferred onto trains which streaked across the conti-

Aerial view of the P. Burns plant, Calgary, ca.1920s

Bill Oliver, right, preparing for aerial photography assignment, ca.1930s

Buffalo being rounded up at Wainwright for shipment to Wood Buffalo Park, ca.1939

Chuckwagon and crew at buffalo roundup, Wainwright, 1929

Bill Oliver being removed from his photographing pit after a thundering buffalo herd had passed over him, 1923

Buffalo crossing Jameson Lake, Wainwright, 1929

nent; all rail traffic was shunted aside to let the silk trains hurtle by. The extremely high value of the silk, from $4 million to $8 million or even $10 million per train, was one reason for the high speed as any delay could cause deterioration of the precious cargo, also the high insurance rates climbed with each passing hour and New York markets were subject to fluctuation.[19] People were intrigued by the flashing trains and their exotic loads so Bill Oliver arranged to make a silk train film. Usually no one was allowed to ride these trains except the crews and the armed guards that patrolled them and how Oliver surmounted this obstacle is not known; possibly his friendship with various CPR officials was a factor. The fact remains that he boarded a silk train with its cargo, shared the excitement of its wild rush across the country, and recorded this phenomenon on film.[20]

In 1921, Bill went to the Buffalo National Park at Wainwright to photograph the buffalo roundup for the Parks Branch. This marked the beginning of a warm and lifelong friendship with E. J. (Bud) Cotton, warden of the park, as well as an extended and often dangerous picture-shooting relationship with that monarch of the plains, the buffalo. Annual buffalo roundups to count the herd and select animals for herd reduction were held in early winter, starting about mid-November and often continuing well into January. Chasing buffalo in winter was hard on men and horses but this was the season for prime hides and the shaggy beasts were prized for the robes they provided.[21]

In 1923 Bill returned to the Wainwright buffalo herd when he was involved with a motion picture named, "The Last Frontier." Thomas H. Ince Studios of Culver City, California, had undertaken to make a movie based on a novel by Courtney Ryley Cooper[22] and for scenes involving buffalo had made an arrangement with the National Parks of Canada. Buffalo for a roundup and stampede were to be provided, park riders were to participate, and permission was given to shoot several head during a simulated buffalo hunt. This was justified because of the necessity of slaughtering a substantial number of animals to reduce the herd to manageable size. Some 150 Cree Indians from the reserves at Hobbema, Alberta, were involved in the action and a campsite for them in the park was part of the agreement. In return the department was to receive financial compensation, surplus cuttings from the films, and extensive free advertising.[23]

In mid-October, 1923, the buffalo park assumed a new role as swarms of actors, Indians and cowboys arrived. There were scenario writers, directors, and a veritable army of cameramen, Oliver numbered among the latter. During the Ince officials' negotiations with Ottawa, W. J. Oliver had been recommended as a photographer with experience in filming buffalo, so he was invited to go to the park as a spare cameraman.[24]

Lines of heavily woven wire fencing were constructed to form a funnel about a mile in length with an entrance a mile wide and narrowing to approximately one hundred yards. Photographers were in camouflaged positions concealed by brush and in pits at strategic points. Bill Oliver and the Ince Company's leading cameraman, Paul Perry, were in a pit in the forefront in the actual path of the buffalo. It had concrete walls and was roofed with steel drums covered with earth from which protuberances projected for the operation of the cameras. Expert riflemen also were concealed in nearby pits. When the riders got the herd in motion some 4,000 head of buffalo thundered down the incline closely pursued by Indian riders and showers of arrows. Buffalo fell as sharp shooters' bullets found their mark; the blunt arrows provided to the Indians caused no wounds but the scene was realistic. The cameramen ground furiously catching on film for the first time not only stampeding buffalo but, it seemed, an Indian buffalo hunt. In the pit where the men crouched, the din of buffalo hooves pounding on the metal drums above was deafening and to say the least, unnerving. However, their shots showing the galloping animals approaching, closer and closer, then leaping overhead, produced spectacular footage. Three separate drives each of around 4,000 head of buffalo were made to secure the scenes required for the movie. On one occasion a buffalo's hind leg crashed in through the top of the shelter, striking Bill's shoulder and completely demolishing his camera. However, he was not badly injured and the exposed film in the camera was undamaged.[25]

Ince was so impressed by Oliver's excellent photography and his fearless attitude towards his work that he offered him a position with the Ince Company in California. The offer was flattering and the substantial salary tempting, but Bill declined.

He felt he would not care to exchange the freedom of the life he led for the confines of a California studio; also his heart was in Canada and he dreamed of owning a ranch in the Alberta foothills.[26]

Bill Oliver continued making periodic photographing trips to the buffalo park; indeed it became customary for him to arrive for the yearly winter roundup. On several occasions he filmed this event for Fox News; not much footage was required but the work often entailed standing at a specified point in 10° or 20°F below zero weather waiting for the herd to appear. Then in 1925 he was again involved in shooting an American commercial film, a Western starring Hoot Gibson. This movie, called "Calgary Stampede," contained footage of a buffalo herd running at top speed. These shots were taken by W.J., the only photographer present who would stand out in the open unprotected while a great buffalo herd thundered past his camera.[27]

Later, about 1929, Bill Oliver undertook the making of his own buffalo film for the Parks Branch. This time the film crew did not resemble a small army. Bill was photographer, director, and scenario writer and his only helpers were the chief warden, Bud Cotton, and eight riders. He decided to again use a camera pit, well reinforced, covered by heavy plank and camouflaged with an aperture left for filming. Once more he ground his camera as a huge herd of buffalo swept down the valley and over the pit. Soil showered in between the planks as great bodies hurtled overhead and the camera recorded some amazing shots until a buffalo cow's foot banged through the aperture. Cotton had seen the cow stumble and as the herd passed he rushed to the pit. There he found that Bill had had the good fortune to miss collision with the hoof but his camera was smashed, although this time not completely wrecked. He took it to Edmonton for repairs and the pit scene was refilmed the following day.[28]

Other spectacular pictures were obtained of buffalo crossing Jameson Lake. This was a natural crossing on the route of an old trail so Bill waited on a raft near some bushes on the north shore as riders started some six hundred head into the lake on the south. They came on the run through water four or more feet deep, exiting near the hidden camera site as Cotton had predicted. However, with their speed and the size of their bodies they drove great waves before them which swamped the raft, tipping its cargo into the now turbulent lake. Bill couldn't swim and desperately clutching his camera he yelled for help. It was a few minutes before the men realized the seriousness of his predicament and hauled him out of the water none the worse for his dipping. Neither Bill Oliver nor Bud Cotton was easily discouraged so heavy posts were driven into the lake shore and a platform built, then the drive was repeated and Bill got some splendid pictures from his elevated position.[29]

A buffalo bull fight was another spectacular sight which was captured in a W. J. Oliver film. One year during the mating season in June or early July when the bulls were challenging each other, Cotton drove the photographer around the park in his open-top Chevy and after witnessing animals engaged in a few minor skirmishes they came across the real thing. Two huge bulls came roaring out of the bush almost beside the truck. Dust, brush and small poplar trees flew around as the great animals tore up the ground and crashed their massive heads together. They were too intent on their battle to notice the little truck where Bill stood cranking his camera, so engrossed in getting the film that Bud Cotton had to hang onto his coattails for fear he'd be down in the middle of the action. Another worry developed when the motor of the Chev died and to start it one had to use the crank. However, before men and vehicle became too embroiled in the action, the fight ended; one bull went down badly gored and as soon as he could regain his feet he retreated with all possible speed.[30]

Bill didn't seek action pictures alone for his film but also took peaceful domestic views of cows with calves, animals wallowing, and general footage depicting the life of the buffalo. There were shots, too, of the elk that shared the buffalo park. The end result was a film called "Home of the Buffalo." It was also the basis of a 1933 production with accompanying sound narrative made for the National Parks Branch by Associated Screen News of Montreal and entitled "The Return of the Buffalo."[31]

In 1925 the Parks Branch commenced a program of shipping young buffalo from the Wainwright to Wood Buffalo Park in the northern Alberta area. It was an exceedingly difficult undertaking. The animals were loaded onto rail cars in Wain-

Grey Owl feeding a baby beaver, ca.1933–34

wright and transported to Waterways via Edmonton. There they were transferred to specially designed barges for travel down the Athabasca and Slave Rivers to the park. During the four years this program was in operation a total of 6,673 buffalo were shipped north.[32] Bill accompanied at least one of these consignments and his photographs illustrated an article on the project by H. H. C. "Torchy" Anderson of the *Calgary Herald*. This story with related pictures received wide distribution, appearing in publications throughout Canada, Britain, and the United States.[33]

Another friendship which had positive results was one which Bill Oliver developed with Grey Owl. Probably the photographer's most noted and best loved movies were those he made of this man and his beavers. He first was commissioned in 1931 by the Parks Branch to produce a movie on the work Grey Owl was doing to conserve beaver.[34] Grey Owl had been a guide and trapper in northern Ontario and Quebec but had turned from killing animals to protecting them. He had found two motherless beaver kittens which he took into his home and it was mainly through the influence of these little animals, McGinnis and McGinty, that he had adopted the life of a naturalist, writer, and conservationist.[35] His work became well known and in 1930 J. C. Campbell of the Parks Branch in company with a cameraman visited him and produced a film showing Grey Owl with his beavers which was entitled "The Beaver People." Soon afterwards the Parks Branch offered him employment, his work to be the conservation of beaver in national parks. He was in Riding Mountain National Park in Manitoba when Bill first met him although shortly he, his Indian wife Anahareo and his beavers were moved to Ajawaan Lake in Prince Albert National Park, Saskatchewan, where conditions were better suited for his purpose.[36]

Bill Oliver's first meeting with Grey Owl was not propitious. He had had to walk the last three miles in to the man's cabin carrying a heavy load on his back and when he got there he was greeted with the brusque statement, "So you're the cameraman. I may as well tell you I have not much use for white men."[37] The reason for this statement, it transpired, was Grey Owl's opinion that most white men wanted to "deface God's earth." Bill sympathized with this feeling for nature but made it clear that his only purpose was to make a movie of the beaver for which he required Grey Owl's full co-operation and should it not be forthcoming he would cancel the project and leave immediately. He added that he would gladly promise not to interfere with the beaver in any manner which did not meet with approval. Grey Owl decided to co-operate. Indeed, as time passed he became very interested in the movie project and gave able assistance. The beavers who were the main characters in the film, Jelly Roll and Rawhide, successors of McGinnis and McGinty in Grey Owl's heart and home, were capricious in their co-operation. Sometimes they performed very well, coming at Grey Owl's call, eating his food or their own bark, playing in the water, grooming themselves, working on their lodge, and generally providing opportunities for marvellous pictures. At other times days passed without them appearing at all and meanwhile Bill waited patiently camera in hand, ignoring flies and mosquitoes, sometimes standing perfectly still waist deep in water. Eventually he had enough footage for a two reel film entitled "The Beaver Family."[38] This was a silent picture but later through the co-operation of Associated Screen News of Montreal a sound version based on the films "The Beaver Family" and "The Beaver People" and called "Grey Owl's Little Brother" was produced.

In subsequent years after Grey Owl's move to Prince Albert Park, Bill paid him further movie making visits. On these occasions his reception was quite different. In April 1933 when plans were underway for a further beaver film, Grey Owl wrote enthusiastically describing a cabin which he was building for use in filming and enclosing a list of suggested shots for the film.[39] The Oliver Grey Owl films were "Pilgrims of the Wild," "Grey Owl's Neighbours," and "Strange Doings in Beaverland." In addition, Associated Screen News produced a sound version of the last-named film and called it "Grey Owl's Strange Guests." The original movies were truly Oliver pictures; he wrote, directed, photographed, and edited them, and they were excellent. They had an appeal and a sincerity which reflected his own feeling for wildlife and the depth of his empathy and understanding of Grey Owl's conservation efforts.[40]

Grey Owl died in 1938 and it was then that the public learned of his masquerade—he was in fact not an Indian but an Englishman named Archibald Belaney. While Bill Oliver was

Grey Owl with moose calves, Riding Mountain National Park, ca.1931

Grey Owl with beaver at Lake Ajawaan, Saskatchewan, ca. 1933–34

making the beaver films, he was in close contact with the man and may have suspected that he was not an Indian, but it would be characteristic of him to respect the other man's choice of a way of life and say nothing. Grey Owl was obviously sincere in his work on the conservation of the beaver, and his contribution in this regard and in the general field of wildlife protection through his writings and lectures was substantial.

Bill Oliver in his own way also contributed to public knowledge and understanding of wildlife. His interest and concern included birds as well as animals. He photographed swans at Nancy Island north-east of Medicine Hat, great blue heron at Leduc, a grey goose with her nest near Calgary, vast flocks of migratory blue and Canada geese on Grant's Lake, Manitoba, and many other birds in their natural habitats.[41] One of his most fascinating bird trips was in 1931 when he heard a somewhat fantastic story about prairie chickens having been observed dancing in the Cypress Hills. From Medicine Hat he was escorted by a local man, Everett Fleming, to the dancing grounds in the hills. After a short wait, as though on cue the birds appeared and commenced their dance. Bill was delighted to see them and with the footage he obtained.[42] Also in 1931 he went to the Pacific coast during the herring spawning season to photograph the sea gulls, cormorants and canvas back ducks. After spawning, the herrings move into deeper water where they are safe from the raiding gulls but ducks in numbers dive for them. The gulls then manage to snatch their share of the feast from the ducks. Bill's bird footage resulted in several fascinating films among which were, "Here and There with the Birds of Canada" and "Fleet Wings."

FILMING IN CANADA'S PARKS

The buffalo and Grey Owl movies which W. J. Oliver filmed for the Parks Branch are indicative of the work he undertook for the Dominion Government in the late twenties and thirties. He first submitted films in addition to still photographs to the branch in the early 1920s as the publicity and information division was interested in adding a library of motion pictures to its pictorial collections. The branch purchased the Waterton Park movie which he shot in 1919.[43] Another early film was made by combining footage taken during his early movie making days and in subsequent years of birds and other wildlife in the parks and this the Parks Branch released under the title, "Sanctuary."[44]

The working arrangement which developed between W. J. Oliver and the Parks Branch was beneficial for all concerned. The director of the publicity division, J. C. Campbell, and later Robert J. C. Stead, would work out with the photographer a proposed schedule, often for a year in advance. They would indicate the parks they wished featured and the type of pictures required. In some instances the film idea originated with W.J. and then was developed after consultation with parks officials. This method of operation gave him unusual freedom as well as responsibility in his movie making. On the basis of his background knowledge, and perhaps a preliminary trip, he wrote a tentative scenario which was then adapted as he shot the required footage. So actually he was script writer, director, cameraman, and sometimes editor, thus in a very real sense these films, although they did not bear his name, were his own creations. The undeveloped negatives were sent to Ottawa where the Parks Branch arranged to have working prints made, first by the Canadian Government Motion Picture Bureau and, commencing in 1927 or 1928, by Associated Screen News in Montreal. W.J. then would spend several weeks in Ottawa working on the film.[45] Titles were usually provided by Parks Branch staff writer, Mabel Williams and, after 1931, Fergus Lothian. Joe Rigby who eventually became head of the moving picture section, also carried out editing and selection of sequences, sometimes in conjunction with W.J., and on occasion assisted by Lothian.[46]

During the twenties and thirties W.J.'s movie and still pictures formed a large part of the department's photographic collection and appeared consistently in parks' publications. From 1925 to 1942 a major proportion of the motion picture film obtained by the Parks Branch was Oliver's work.[47] Through this period the branch's print and film libraries were extensively used as they offered free accesssibility of the material for public use. This resulted in greatly increased public awareness, use and enjoyment of national parks; Bill Oliver's unique wildlife and action coverage, his superb quality photographs and films, were a decided factor in this achieve-

Overlooking Waterton Lakes, 1934. Left to right are Harold Long, of the Lethbridge Herald, Marjorie and Joan Oliver.

ment.[48] In return the broad exposure of his work undoubtedly extended and enhanced his already firm reputation as a photographer, and through the branch he was assured of steady and lucrative employment during the lean years of the Depression.

From Bill's early days in Calgary the Rocky Mountains had had for him a magnetic attraction and now he explored to the full their motion picture film possibilities. Probably the first mountain films he sold went to Fox News but before long the Parks Branch displayed a keen interest in his Rocky Mountain movies and provided a ready market. Quite likely the earliest films of the Banff area which he supplied to the branch were of the travelogue type. A picture entitled "Banff" and dated tentatively 1929 shows visitors arriving at the station and being driven to see the buffalo paddocks, hoodoos, fish hatchery, zoo, Banff Springs Hotel, and along the Tunnel Mountain drive. The tourists are then pictured canoeing, golfing, swimming, and generally enjoying the facilities of the resort. A more ambitious travel film made about 1930 covered a motor trip from Spokane to Banff and was named "Through Mountain Gateways."

However, Bill Oliver's best known mountain pictures were his spectacular high country action productions and his wildlife movies. Skiing was an integral part of the life in the region so Bill learned the sport and accompanied skiers even on their most difficult runs. He also joined the Alpine Club in 1919 or 1920 and became an active member in 1927, thus gaining greater facility in climbing, a familiarity with mountaineering procedures, and a place among the Alpine fraternity. His friends included Swiss guides Rudolf Aemmer, Christian Hasler, Ernest Feuz, and many local pack train outfitters and guides. Besides enjoying their company Bill had the highest respect for the men who guided his photographic expeditions. Despite his desire to get the best pictures possible and propensity for taking chances, when on the trail he unhesitatingly accepted his guides' decisions. He always claimed that to them must go much credit for the noted mountain and wildlife pictures he was able to get. He contended that on many occasions his life was saved by the forethought and direct action of his guides.[47] For mountain photography, everyone involved needed strength and stamina as well as courage. The

Georgia Engelhard and Swiss guide Ernest Feuz on Mount Victoria, 1933

Punchbowl Falls in Jasper National Park

camera which Bill carried on his back on these mountain trips weighed fifty-five pounds, the tripod was another fifty pounds but was usually packed by a guide.[50]

"She Climbs to Conquer" was a noteworthy film which gained well merited acclaim. Made in 1933 it pictured the climb of Georgia Engelhard, a professional mountain climber, from Abbot's Pass to the peak of Mount Victoria. Ernest Feuz was Miss Engelhard's guide and Rudolph Aemmer acted in the same capacity for Oliver. They started from the chalet at Lake Louise and made their base the hut on top of Abbot's Pass. From there the attack of Mount Victoria was launched. Actually to obtain the footage Bill desired, it was necessary to spend nine days in climbing; the mountain was scaled seven times. This was the first time a standard moving picture outfit had reached the top of Mount Victoria. The ascent was not easy and Bill's greatest difficulty was finding secure and suitable locations from which to photograph the climber. He wanted shots which would establish height and depth and indicate the steepness of the climb. He also required spots level enough upon which to stand the tripod. On one instance the guides lowered him by rope over a precipice onto a ledge which provided the right angle and footing.

At another point in his climb, a chain of rock gendarmes barred their way. From there it was an almost vertical drop of 2,000 feet towards Lake O'Hara while on the Lake Louise side on Upper Victoria Glacier they faced a huge crevasse some 1,000 feet in depth. However, the crossing was made safely and when they reached the peak its commanding position rewarded them with a magnificent view in all directions.[51] On the way back the guides noted a storm coming so Miss Engelhard and her guide hurried on towards the hut but Aemmer and Bill Oliver remained on the ridge as the latter wanted to photograph the spectacular skies that heralded the approaching storm. Suddenly the wind hit with hurricane force and Bill found himself clinging desperately to his camera and the rock face. Then followed a terrific electrical storm with torrential rain and great crashes of thunder. Lightning flashed around them—it came with a strange sizzling noise, sparks flew from the ice axes, the hair on the men's heads lifted and crackled, and the air was heavy with the smell of sulphur. They finally managed to take shelter under some overhanging rocks until

Trail ride to Mount Wedgewood, 1936

the storm abated. It was the worst electrical storm either man had experienced; not even Aemmer with his extensive mountain work had seen its equal.[52]

Around this period or earlier, arrangements were made for Bill Oliver and his camera to join Jack Brewster, the noted guide and outfitter, for a pack horse trip from Lake Louise to Jasper. With filming stops it became a twenty-two day journey. One of the problems en route was the crossing of rivers. Hot summer weather causing melting snow and glacial ice had resulted in rising rivers and after some heavy mountain rains these became rushing torrents. The Saskatchewan River near the base of Mount Murchison was very high and even though the party waited a day until it had subsided somewhat, the horses had to swim across and men and packs alike received a thorough wetting. Eventually they reached the main objective of the trip, the Columbia ice fields. This immense pack of ice forms the main source of both the North and South Saskatchewan Rivers, the Athabasca and is a part of the watershed that supplies the Columbia River system. Bill was greatly impressed and spent four days filming the area for a movie which was appropriately entitled "Cradle of Rivers." The party then climbed Mount Castleguard which provided a remarkable view of surrounding mountains and afforded more excellent footage for the film. After the ice field was transversed, their trail led through Wilcox Pass and along the Sunwapta River to the Athabasca, and on to Jasper townsite.[53] It had been an arduous trip but the result was another fine film.

Bill always contended that it was on this trip that he managed to infect his friend Jack Brewster with his "camera-hunting disease." He argued about the merits of shooting with a camera as opposed to a gun and talked of the gratification of capturing a wild animal on film. As a result he and Jack Brewster spent most of the late summer and fall of that year photographing wildlife in Jasper National Park. These trips converted Jack Brewster, and Bill Oliver, who had never been an avid hunter but over the years had indulged in some duck and game bird shooting, now hung his gun on the wall, a gesture of finality to which he remained true.

Much of the footage obtained at that time was included in a film produced for the Parks Branch, "Hunting Without a Gun."[54] This picture is highlighted by a truly remarkable sequence of close views of a grizzly bear. Jack Brewster had found a trail which he said was frequented by a grizzly. Bill always accepted without question his friend's knowledge of the woods and wild animal's habits, so the two men confidently planned a lure for the bear. They built a blind to conceal

Trail riders camp with Mount Assiniboine in background, 1936

themselves and the cameras; next, at varying distances from their hideout they placed bait in the form of fresh meat. Waiting was part of the pattern involved in wildlife photography so this phase was customary procedure for Bill. On this occasion he was fortunate in having company in his blind for it wasn't until the seventh day that the bear appeared. Bill had dozed off, but immediately was wide awake and within seconds his cine-camera was in action; Brewster was already busily photographing with a smaller one. The bear, a giant grizzly, over a thousand pounds in weight they estimated, was sniffing at the nearest bait, just thirty-five feet away. He left, then returned and started eating the meat. This, a fairly large piece of an animal carcass, the bear attacked voraciously, shortly jerking it loose from its stake and dragging it into the bush out of sight. A few minutes later he appeared at a more distant bait which he quickly finished and moved off, only to reappear at a third lure, this time some sixty feet away. After his third visit all was quiet. There were two more baits but the bear seemed to have gone. The cameras had ground furiously all the time the animal was within range and the men congratulated themselves on the phenomenal footage they must have taken.

Suddenly they were shaken by the realization after the fact of the extreme danger they had been in. They had a standing rule that no liquor should be drunk while on the trail, but Bill had a flask for use in emergencies. He got it out; this surely was an emergency. Just then Brewster motioned him to look behind. There not a hundred yards away stood the grizzly, eyeing them. Evidently something had aroused his suspicions and he had circled, catching the scent, not only of humans but of the other two baits. Now the men were between grizzly and the meat. Just as the bear charged, Bill Oliver and Jack Brewster grabbed their cameras and were on their way; they never made better time. Fortunately, for them, the bear stopped for the bait, so his live quarries got away safely.[55]

"Hunting Without a Gun" was an exciting picture to see and the stories behind it were as dramatic as anything fiction could produce. This film is credited with stimulating interest in North America in photographing wild animals, notably game animals. Another movie made a little later reinforced the camera hunting theme. This one, also a National Parks production, was named, "Stalking Big Game" and sought to show that animal pictures could be taken by other than professional photographers. Dan Byck, a big game hunter from Louisville, Texas, and Jack Brewster, guide, were the human characters in this film. Byck, under Brewster's guidance, set off from Jasper to hunt moose, caribou, black bear, goats, Rocky .Mountain sheep and other animals, armed only with his camera. Oliver meanwhile filmed the men travelling, Byck photographing, and the animals he was shooting with his camera.[56] Again some hair-raising incidents occurred and some excellent animal shots were obtained.

In the spring of 1932 Bill Oliver made one of his most popular skiing pictures, "Skiing in Cloudland" and recorded his activities in considerable detail. During late March he filmed around Lake Louise despite most adverse weather while in the following month he had to go home to recuperate after a mountain "spill" which had resulted in "a slight fracture of the ankle bone, plus water on the knee."[57] By 28 April he was back at Lake Louise ready for an ascent of Fossil Mountain. The party included Peter and Catharine Whyte, well-known ski and mountain enthusiasts; Mrs. Barbara White, also of Banff; Norman Knight, Banff skier; and Vic Kuschera, a professional ski jumper and ski instructor at Skoki. The first part of the trip from Lake Louise to the Skoki Valley ski camp was made by dog team, then they ascended via Ptarmigan Valley to Deception Pass between Fossil Mountain and Pike's Peak. There was a great depth of snow and the climb was difficult. Often when Bill got off his skis to set up his tripod he would sink hip deep in the soft snow. Again there were occasions when he had to be lowered over ledges to get the camera position for the shots he desired of the ascending or descending skiers. Another problem was sunburn. The weather was unreasonably hot and the sun's rays reflected a burning glare from the dazzling whiteness of the snow; even though protective masks were worn some badly burned faces resulted. Despite the discomfort there was great beauty on the mountainside and later Bill described the scenes in poetic terms. At times, he said, "the vista was fairy-like in the delicacy of its colouring" and he spoke of "a golden cascade of light reflecting a kaleidoscope aura more lovely than a rainbow in June."[58]

About three years later the Parks Branch had a sound version of "Skiing in Cloudland" produced by Associated

Screen News which they called "Let's Go Skiing." After this, Bill made another skiing picture set in Sunshine Valley which was entitled "Sunshine and Powder-Snow."

One early Oliver picture taken in Banff National Park was filmed from the air and named, "Over the Top of the Canadian Rockies." The plane flew down the valley south of Banff then turned westward and circled over Mount Assiniboine. Bill found the sea of mountains truly spectacular. The terrain looked flatter from a higher altitude and he wanted to catch the mountains in their true magnificence, so the pilot flew as low as he dared and both men disregarded the risks.[59]

In 1928 Bill Oliver again produced a film of Waterton Lakes National Park. In it his wife Marjorie, her sister-in-law, Jem Martin, and Vic Valentine of Calgary were shown riding, hiking, golfing, boating, admiring the scenery and generally illustrating the tourist attractions of the park. David Cromarty, son of the acting superintendent, also appeared in the film.[60] Bill liked having his family and friends participate in these movies; he felt that their approach to riding, camping, and other activities resulted in a naturalness which would not be evident in a production with professional actors and actresses.

A further Waterton Lakes film as an update for tourists was made in 1934. In this instance Marjorie and their daughter Joan, then just thirteen, were joined by Harold G. Long, editor of the *Lethbridge Herald* and close friend of the Olivers, in portraying the action for the picture. The story begins in Lethbridge as the party, presumably tourists, visits the highlights of the city, also the Mormon temple at Cardston, before motoring on to Waterton. Here the usual camping and related outdoor activities are shown while the facilities of the resort and the grandeur of surrounding scenery are given full treatment.[61]

Joan was the principal in another of her father's pictures made in 1936. This, a mountain climbing film, was designed mainly to show the might of Mount Assiniboine, at this period sometimes referred to as "the Canadian Matterhorn." The plan was to climb Mount Wedgewood, and much of the footage taken there would show the forbidding Assiniboine. Joan was accustomed to hiking but had not previously attempted mountain climbing. She enjoyed outdoors activities and shared something of her father's feeling for the mountains, also she was always excited by the prospect of being in his pictures and of participating with him in the experience of a filming trip.

It was decided that she should have a trial run, so on 21 June, leaving from Lake Louise with guides Chris Hasler and Rudolph Aemmer, Joan and Bill climbed up to Lake Agnes and from there ascended the Needles. Joan managed well so both her father and her guide, Chris Hasler, agreed she could attempt Mount Wedgewood. Bill hired one of Brewster's pack outfits with a wrangler and cook, and a few days later the party left Banff heading for Assiniboine. They were two days on the trail and then at their Assiniboine camp for about two weeks as rain delayed the climb. Eventually the weather co-operated and the ascent of Mount Wedgewood was made.[62] Joan acquitted herself very well and the ensuing film, "In the Shadow of Mount Assiniboine" was another successful production for the national parks. In August of that year Bill was filming at Louisbourg, Nova Scotia, when he wrote to Joan, saying that word from Ottawa indicated that the Assinboine picture was being well received and congratulating and warmly thanking her again for the work she did for him in this picture, adding, "You sure were a brick."[63]

In 1941 the other two daughters, Doreen and A.J., had their opportunity to appear in an Oliver film. This was a travelogue production with Lake O'Hara as its focal point. With their father the girls drove to Radium, then visited Field, Takakkaw Falls, Emerald Lake, Yoho; they rode with one of the wardens, hiked and climbed, eventually reaching Lake O'Hara. It was a ten day trip and for the girls an experience to remember.[64]

Bill Oliver's sports productions also captured the rhythm of movement of hikers, skiers, skaters, and canoists; they portrayed the feeling of conflict as climbers pitted their skill against the impregnability of mountains; they revealed the determination, the exhilaration, and the sense of achievement of the participants.

Not all his action pictures taken in the national park dealt with sports. The branch's program of road building continued after the opening of the Banff-Windermere Highway in 1923 and Bill followed its progress on film. In fact often he traversed the route first and his photographs helped to indicate its path and to publicize the proposed road. For example, in 1925 he took pictures of the terrain through which the Lake Louise to

Night camp near Maligne Lake, ca.1930s

Joan Oliver and guide Chris Hasler viewing Mount Assiniboine from the slopes of Mount Wedgewood, 1936

Georgia Engelhard and Swiss guide Ernest Feuz ascending Mount Victoria, 1933

Golden road would pass, views of the Yoho Valley, the Great Divide, and the Kicking Horse Canyon, including one showing where the road would cross the Kicking Horse. The portion of the road from Lake Louise to Field was scheduled to open in the spring of 1926 and the Field to Golden link was planned for the following year.[65] Later he filmed the actual construction.

During the Depression years the government followed a policy of combining the construction of roads in the parks with their unemployment relief work plan and as a result, road building in the parks expanded greatly. One of the most ambitious of the new roads was the Big Bend highway which extended west of Golden, following the great curve of the Columbia River. Bill took photographs and film footage of its construction. His pictures, such as a series of stills taken in September 1931, illustrate graphically the struggle of man and horse power against the force of forests, mountains, and rivers.[66]

For a time he worked with the surveyors at the head of the line in heavily timbered country, where he could secure shots of the loggers felling the giant trees. After them came the powder man to blast the massive roots out before graders and scoops could work on the road bed. Although Bill would have his camera set up in a supposedly safe location he once narrowly missed being hit by a huge descending mass of roots and soil. On another occasion a great rock had to be dynamited out in a "side-hill gouging" operation. Holes drilled by compressors penetrated the rock and the thirty fuses inserted were connected to the firing battery situated near the camera position. For this operation the chief engineer had had a rough shack covered with wooden slabs and old galvanized roofing constructed and in here Bill had set up his camera. A Mounted Policeman on the site to monitor the dynamiting joined him. When the plunger went down Bill was cranking his camera. The explosion came with a mighty earth-shaking roar; this was followed a few seconds later by a nerve-shattering din as fragments of rock rained down on the metal roof of the shelter. Meanwhile the volume of rock falling into the river backed up the water creating a great spraying wash. Fortunately there was no injury nor damage but the experience resulted in a tense and exciting few minutes.[67] The Big Bend highway proved to be a dangerous and herculean undertaking but the finished road formed an important link in the all-Canadian route from the Great Lakes to the Pacific coast. It was offiically opened on 29 June 1940.[68]

Other unemployment relief work projects resulted in improvement of the Banff-Windermere highway, the construction of the Banff-Jasper road, the rebuilding of the road from the southern boundary of Prince Albert National Park, Saskatchewan, to the headquarters, the reconstruction of the main road across Riding Mountain National Park, Manitoba, and the building of a new link up the face of the escarpment from Neepawa.[69] During construction of these routes, the photographer and his camera would appear to mark the event.

Bill Oliver was a strong man but the physical demands of movie making in the mountains during this period were so great that at times the effort took its toll. On one occasion when he was filming in the Amethyst Lakes area one leg became swollen and very painful. It had bothered him for some days but he had disregarded it and continued his scramble over rough terrain. However, when he reached base camp on the completion of the work his leg was swollen to the knee and his boot had to be cut off. The leg was bandaged and given some support and in the morning he was hoisted into the saddle to start the long painful ride out. They caught the train at a flag point and the remainder of the trip to Jasper was easier to bear. The doctor diagnosed the trouble as inflammatory rheumatism and ordered a long rest.[70]

For Bill a worry in mountain travel was the safety of his cameras. When on the trail they were loaded on one of the pack ponies. One morning when starting on a trip in Jasper National Park there was a sudden commotion and a pack pony took off at a full gallop into the woods. Bill yelled and dashed in pursuit on foot. In a few minutes he reached the pony which had collided with a tree, shattering the pack. He had visions of ruined cameras and smashed lenses but he was relieved to find a mass of broken eggs. The stores had been in this pack and the other grey pony carried his cameras.

Not all the Oliver mountain pictures were action packed; some were quite different in concept and mood. An example is "Jasper of the Lakes," a picturization of a poem of the same name by T. P. O'Connor, a Jasper school teacher, which portrayed the beauties of Jasper National Park in each season

View of Waterton townsite, 1934

of the year.[71]

Other specialized pictures were those dealing with fishing. Bill was always an enthusiastic fisherman. It was to him both an enjoyable sport and a means of relaxation, so he combined it with the type of work he liked best and made fishing movies. "With Lure and Line in Jasper" released in 1932 shows his good friend, Dr. J. G. Gunn of Calgary, fishing in Maligne Lake, Jasper, and about 1935 he filmed "Angling in the Infinite," in which amateur anglers, including his daughter Joan and Swiss guides, Chris Hasler and Rudolph Aemmer, fished for trout in Marvel Lake, Banff National Park.

From the early 1920s on, the beauties, activities and the wildlife of neighbouring British Columbia attracted Bill Oliver. As early as 1922 he filmed a lavish pageant which marked the official opening of the reconstruction of David Thompson's Kootenae House in the Lake Windermere district.[72] Possibly this was a Fox News production. In 1927 he made a film for Fox on the laying of the deep sea cable, focusing on its landing at Bamfield, Vancouver Island. Then when the story of the Hudson's Bay Company's post at Fort St. James, B.C., was commemorated by a pageant in September 1928, Bill was there photographing the event for Fox News.

Predictably, too, the fishing facilities in the province appealed to him and provided numerous opportunities for producing fishing films and indulging in a bit of the sport. He spent about ten days during the last part of May 1935, in the Kamloops area photographing anglers, one of whom was his friend Torchy Anderson, now of the *Vancouver Sun*. Some of the best footage showed fly fishing for Kamloops trout.[73] This footage was included in the resultant National Parks film, "Where Fighting Beauties Rise." Tyee salmon fishing on Campbell River was the subject of another tourist promotional film taken in 1933 for the parks. The occasion was the Tyee Fishing Club's annual contest and members with their catches appeared in the movie.

Vancouver Island was familiar ground for Bill Oliver as he had made numerous pictures there over the years. In June 1931, he took film footage of the Forbidden Plateau, some 140 miles north of Victoria. Going in from Courtenay with some local hikers, they used pack horses part of the way then hiked onto the heavily snow clad plateau. It was a fascinating place with overtones of mystery. According to an Indian legend a group of old men, women, and children of the Comox tribe had been sent onto the plateau for safety while the warriors battled the Cowichans. When the victorious Comox returned to the plateau their people had vanished leaving no trace. Consequently this was regarded as forbidden territory into which no Comox Indian would venture.[74] Bill was not concerned about the legend but there was another unusual phenomenon which he found most interesting. While on the plateau the party visited the red snow area. Here in wide veins some six feet deep, the snow looked decidedly red. The travellers picked up handfuls, some from deep within the vein, yet when examined this way it appeared perfectly white. It was a baffling experience.[75] Nevertheless Bill was enthusiastic about the beauties and tourist attractions of the plateau, being particularly impressed by Cruickshank Canyon.[76]

During the early 1930s, the Director of Publicity of the Parks Branch, in an effort to escape the unpleasant winter weather in Ontario, spent most of the season in Victoria and Vancouver where he lectured and showed slides extolling the attractions of national parks. Coastal publicity bureaus supported his programs and a co-operative relationship developed with such bodies, particularly the Victoria and Island Publicity Bureau. This resulted in the production of motion pictures funded by the Parks Branch which advertised the scenic attractions and sports opportunities on the island.[77] Bill Oliver, the photographer involved, worked closely with George I. Warren, commissioner of the bureau, in documenting on film the island's beauties and capturing the flavour of its personality. The most noted of his island pictures were "Island of Enchantment," in 1930 and "Canada's Evergreen Playground," 1934. The arrangement was that copies were provided for the island's publicity bureau, and Commissioner Warren, who became known as "Mister Victoria" showed the films far and wide in his energetic programs of tourist promotion.

Undoubtedly Bill's most daring and difficult filming project in British Columbia was the production in 1935 of "Sea Lions of the Pacific." The plan was to visit the great rookeries of the sea lions located on small islands, actually precipitous outcroppings of rocks, beyond the northern tip of Vancouver Island. These rocks were exposed to the might of the sea and wind and could be approached only in the calmest of weather. Even then breakers rolled in constantly and landing on the slippery rocks was extremely dangerous.

Parks officials thought a movie of the sea lions would be wonderful but such an undertaking had never before been attempted and some people declared it was impossible; however, Bill Oliver was willing to try. In June, he sailed from Nanaimo on the Fisheries Department's ship, *Givenchy* and two days later they were in Queen Charlotte Sound standing off the Virgin Rocks. Because of rocks and rip tides the *Givenchy* could not approach the sea lions' islands so a twenty-foot powered dinghy had been readied for the task. It had special steel plates clamped to the bow to withstand ramming the rocks and was equipped with a platform covered by coconut matting to provide footing behind which stood a strong post. Bill and his helper, who assisted in carrying equipment and providing protection, landed one at a time. The procedure was to stand on the platform clinging to the post as the dinghy rushed towards the shore on the crest of a huge wave, then at the right second to jump onto the rocks and hang on. The next instant the boat was about ten feet below and retreating. With heavy equipment strapped on their backs it was difficult to scramble up the slippery rocks, and always there was danger that the sea lions might make for the water by the same route they were taking. Nevertheless they landed and Bill started his photographing. For almost two weeks the project continued; on many days landing was impossible but the most was made of all opportunities. He filmed the animals on the Virgin Rocks several times and also on the Haycocks where the creatures swarmed by the thousands. At this season the young of the sea lions were still quite helpless and the cows, great animals weighing about five hundred pounds, were usually ferocious in protecting them. The bulls were huge, about 1,500 pounds in weight, and unpredictable in their behaviour. Bill got shots of them on the rocks and in the sea, of cows threatening an invader or playing with their young, of the pups learning to swim or having mock battles. It was marvellous footage and he felt it was worth the danger and the discomforts, even that of enduring the extremely strong unpleasant smell that permeated the rookeries.[78] However, it was a feat that was not to be attempted again.[79]

A special bonus of the expedition was a chance sighting of a school of basking sharks and later one of sperm whales. Bill was able to obtain excellent shots of these later creatures, thus making a valuable addition to his sea life film footage.

Moving eastward, Prince Albert National Park in Saskatchewan was another favoured locale for Oliver films. In addition to his work with Grey Owl, Bill produced pictures designed to promote the recreational facilities of the park. For example, a group of young people who were camping, canoeing, and generally enjoying the park co-operated with him in producing a movie. He liked to use young people in his films and had no difficulty in establishing rapport with them. "Health and Recreation in Prince Albert National Park" was one of his popular pictures of this area.

Other Parks Branch assignments took him to Riding Mountain National Park in Manitoba. "Playgrounds of the Prairie" was one film which resulted from his movie work here. Also he undertook various filming commissions in the Maritimes. In addition to sport fishing coverage his most extensive work here was the making of promotional films of the Cabot Trail. "The Highlands of Cape Breton" resulted from his work in 1936 and later, probably in 1939, he made the film "Along the Cabot Trail."

The last mentioned picture was filmed in 16 mm colour. Bill kept abreast of new developments in his profession and undoubtedly had been following the results of experimentation in colour photography. Sometime in the early 1930s he decided to enter the field himself and went to New York to study the techniques. There he worked for several months with a colour photographer, Alvin Wyckoff.[80] However, the first colour picture he submitted to the Parks Branch was not accepted.[81] The department at that time had not ventured into colour film, but Bill persevered and in 1937 sold the branch a colour picture, its first.[82]

In 1937, Robert J. C. Stead, who following a reorganization of the parks information services had succeeded J. C. Campbell as supervisor of the area, sent an enthusiastic telegram to Oliver about his new Prince Albert National Park motion pictures, both black and white and colour, just received, describing the colour pictures as excellent.[83] This was the picture "Colourful Days in Prince Albert National Park." "Playgrounds

Picnickers at Paignton Beach, Prince Albert National Park, ca.1930s

Rural view in the Maritimes, 1936

View of Mount Rundle and Vermilion Lakes, 1930s. Marjorie Oliver and Vic Valentine in the car.

of the Prairie" featuring Riding Mountain National Park was also in colour and around the same period Bill refilmed Waterton Park, this time in colour and including scenes on the Chief Mountain International Highway from Glacier National Park, Montana, producing a picture named, "Playground of Two Nations." Bill liked filming in colour. He had a strong feeling for life and realism in his work and probably the depth and variation provided by colour appealed to him. He made colour pictures of some of his favourite mountain and other haunts and wanted to do more; indeed, he had a dream of refilming in colour all his major pictures, but this he recognized as a dream.[84]

Sound pictures, too, became a part of the Parks Branch film library. In these, silent films were adapted for sound through having an announcer record an appropriate narrative which was then merged with the silent footage. This did not involve Bill directly as the procedure was carried out by Associated Screen News of Montreal.[85] However, quite a number of Oliver pictures were chosen for this sound adaptation process.

The parks motion picture business which had flourished throughout the thirties came to a halt during World War Two. It revived briefly in the mid-forties but in 1947 all Parks Branch motion picture films, of which there were some eighty-five, with all negatives and projection equipment, were transferred to the National Film Board.[86]

For approximately two decades Bill Oliver had carried out camera work for the Park Branch and during this time he had travelled untold thousands of miles. Not only did his assignments take him criss-crossing Canada by train but he traversed and retraversed the parks themselves, travelling by motor, airplane, canoe, saddle horse, and dog team, and in addition he covered many miles hiking, skiing, mountain climbing, and snowshoeing. His familiarity with Canada's national parks could scarcely have been rivalled.

Banff townsite, from Stoney Squaw Mountain, 1920s

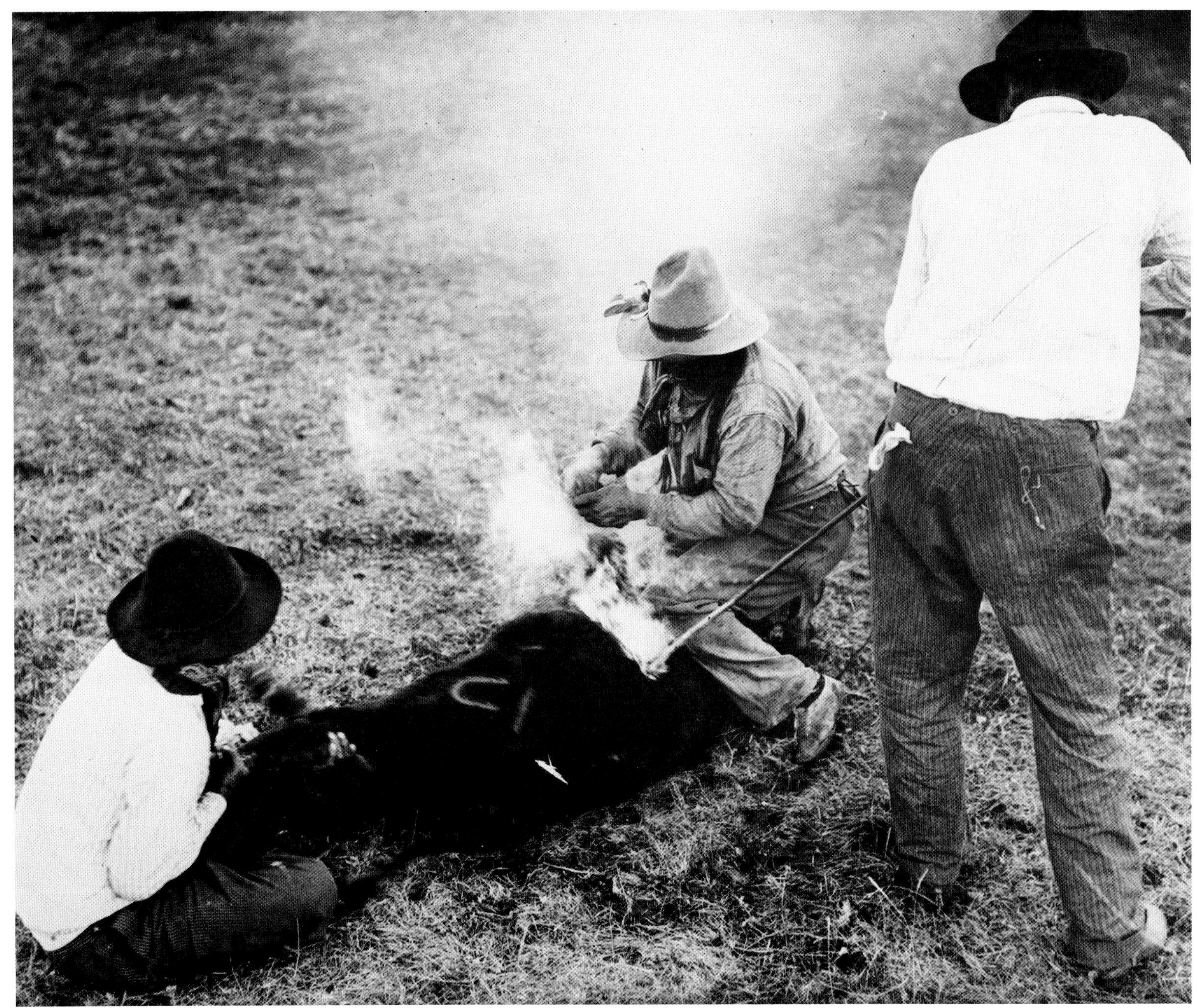

Branding at the Bar U Ranch, ca.1919

V. Ranching and Safaris

In 1933 Bill Oliver realized a dream of many years—he bought land for a ranch in the Alberta foothills. The area chosen was the Millarville district approximately thirty-two miles southwest of Calgary, country which he had known and loved since he commenced visiting the Knights family there during the early teens.

This decisive step taken in the depth of the Depression undoubtedly resulted only after much thought and discussion. The Olivers liked outdoor life, and the advantage to the girls of living in the country would outweigh the disadvantages. In addition there was Bill's long time desire to own a ranch and raise cattle. Economically, while the initial outlay might loom large, Bill planned to continue with his work; also the ranch business when developed would be a hedge against the Depression. Studio work declined in times of short money and Bill realized that he would not always be able to withstand the rigours of outdoor action film making. It seemed a good move to make and the girls were excited at the thought of living in the country.

The Olivers had obtained a cottage at Sylvan Lake in 1930 and the family spent parts of holidays and weekends there. Often on Friday afternoons, even during the winter, Bill and Marjorie would pick up the children at Sunalta School and the family would head north for the hundred-mile trip to their cottage, eating a supper of sandwiches en route. It was fun at the lake with skating or swimming in accordance with the season, but its attractions paled at the prospect of life on their own ranch.

Bill Oliver's initial purchase, land originally settled by John McKinnon, consisted of nearly 740 acres, bounded on the north and mainly the east by a large curve of the North Fork of Sheep River. The land was good and its location appealing but a house site with access to the main road was required, a necessity for a man who would be driving to Calgary every day. The question was solved through the purchase from Mrs. E. Fisher of a small acreage of land running west of the property. This included an attractive building site with a beautiful mountain view and easy access to the Millarville-Black Diamond road. Although the price, $20 per acre, was high for the times, Bill bought the piece of property. In 1937 he added more land on the north side of the river bought from Malcolm T. Millar, thus obtaining a ranch of slightly over 1,100 acres.[1]

A house was the first requirement and Bill discovered that the Royalite Oil Company in Turner Valley was disposing of a number of large bunk houses from its camp which he felt would answer this need. With the economy in its depressed state, such buildings were not saleable so the company was prepared to make them available to anyone willing to pay for their removal. Bill hired a trucker in the oilfields area to haul seven bunk houses to his Millarville land at a cost of $50 each. Of these he planned to use two large bunk houses for the family home, two for a house for the foreman, two for barns, and a smaller one for a storage area. The buildings were structurally sound but required a great deal of work, wall finishing, interior design and renovation to make them usable. With the help of a Lancashire carpenter the bunk houses were converted into functional livable units and the big house emerged as a fine residence.

The house planned for a ranch foreman and his family was the first part of the project undertaken and when the family moved to the ranch in May 1933, they lived there temporarily. It was only partly completed and the confusion resulting from living in a house still under construction was unsettling. One day Marjorie discovered her youngest daughter, seven-year-old Audrey Jean, sitting on a box in the midst of partially-emptied packing cases, crying disconsolately. When Marjorie went to comfort her, the child asked tearfully, "When are we going home?" This incident caused her parents to wonder if in fact the ranch move was in the best interests of the children. However, as the buildings began to take their projected shape, and Bill and Marjorie managed to bring order out of chaos, the sense of confusion and disorientation dissapated. Before long A.J. had adjusted to her new surroundings. She spent many happy hours sitting on bunk house floors busily extracting coins from between the floor boards, relics of the poker games which had formed the main entertainment of the men who had called the bunk houses home in the Royalite camp.[2] As her store of silver grew she felt she was attaining great wealth. When the interiors of the buildings were torn apart the other girls, too, became involved in this lucrative sport of finding coins.

When finished, the Oliver house lent itself admirably to entertaining and indeed this had been one of the factors in its design. The bunk houses were transformed into a comfortable and attractive home. The house set on a basement was L-shaped with each of the two bunk houses forming a wing. One consisted of four bedrooms opening off a long hall, and the kitchen, dining room and living room comprised the other, while a bathroom and square shaped hall connected the two. A verandah was built along the north side of the house. The living room, large and almost square, featured a picture window to the west that presented a view of rolling hills and mountains, ever changing, ever lovely. A big stone fireplace on the north wall formed the interior focal point. In anticipation of a fireplace some of the stones had been picked up previously in the mountains but the majority were found along Sheep Creek. In the centre was a small but interesting piece of quartz that Bill had discovered on one of his mountain trips. Another memorable stone he had carried by pack pony over the Kicking Horse Pass when photographing prior to the road survey.

An exciting project which all the girls enjoyed was learning to ride. Joan felt embarrassed that she, a girl of some twelve years, had little knowledge of how to ride or handle a horse, so she was determined to remedy the situation with all possible speed. Doreen, too, was anxious to learn this new skill that went with living on a ranch, and A.J. was ready to follow her sisters' lead. Flash, a large and venerable bay gelding, gentle but with fixed ideas, had come with the place. He looked immensely tall, as a horse of a sixteen or seventeen hands does to children unaccustomed to riding, but they discovered, when their father wasn't there to boost them onto his back, that by mounting an apple box perched on top of a broken chair they were able to scramble up. The horse's habit of making for the barn when a child landed on his back was frightening at first but they persevered and through much practise, and coaching from their father, they soon acquired a sense of balance

Bill Oliver at his Diamond L Ranch, ca.1930s

and learned the rudiments of horsemanship.

Another of Bill's early priorities was the commencement of his cattle business. He had specific knowledge of the attributes of beef animals and had absorbed much ranch lore through his friendly association with cattlemen that had resulted from his work as the ranchman's photographer, but he realized that he was entering a field that was new to him. He sought advice from a close friend, Harold Long, editor of the *Lethbridge Herald*. Agriculture was in the editor's background through his Ontario farm upbringing and by association with his brother's ranch in the Longview area south of Turner Valley, but it was mainly through his newspaper work that he had gained a considerable store of knowledge of the agricultural scene. He became extremely interested in the ranch project; he was always ready with advice concerning the availability of good cattle, the best types of hay and grains to grow, and beef feeding policies.

The first range cattle purchase was some sixty head of young Hereford cows from the McIntyre Ranch in southern Alberta. These animals, the nucleus of the breeding herd, were good stock and Bill consistently followed a policy of buying first class animals, thus building up a good beef herd. For his brand, he originally chose the middle letters of his name, LIV, which he registered in March 1933, but found this too large as it covered much of a calf's side. He then obtained a two symbol brand in July 1934, the Diamond L, a good brand, neat and distinctive that didn't blotch easily nor lend itself to alteration.[3] As time passed the ranch was referred to as the Diamond L.

With the acquisition of stock came the need for ranch hands. Bill's photographic profession remained his first priority and took the bulk of his time, so he hired a foreman. Other men were taken on as required and soon after acquiring his property he hired Sarcee Indians to pick roots.

During their first years on the ranch when the house construction and renovation was underway, Marjorie and Bill Oliver were particularly busy as there were various aspects of this work which they carried out themselves. Then, too, there was the landscaping and work in the garden.

The Olivers were a busy family but they had time for fun and relaxation. A favorite pastime was riding. The first saddle horse obtained was a chestnut named Sunshine purchased for Marjorie from Mike Knights. Pete and Freckles were two early acquisitions, but the girls, now enthusiastic riders, wanted their own horses. In 1934 there was great excitement over the arrival from Pincher Creek of a grey mare bought for Joan from Mrs. J. Holroyd. She was called Radium, Rady for short. Later Doreen became the proud owner of a horse called Sailor and A.J.'s special horse was Ponjola. These three mares, the foals they produced, and other horses on the ranch brought the girls great pleasure and added an important dimension to their lives. Their father bought a saddle horse for himself later. He said he didn't want one that was always ready to race like the spirited horses the rest of the family liked. He wanted a good, reliable cow pony, and eventually he purchased Danny. A rather homely dark bay, drab in appearance, he proved to be the good cow pony Bill was seeking.

The girls attended a rural school and this they found to be disconcerting at first because of being teased as "city girls," but, as they soon learned to hold their own and earned acceptance, they found the experience rewarding. They started in September 1933 walking a mile and a half across the fields to New Valley School. At times in winter when the snow was too deep or crusted or the temperature dipped well below zero, one of the men from the ranch would arrive with a team and sleigh to drive the children home. By their second year on the Diamond L they were riding to school and feeling truly a part of the ranch country life. This was the era when girls wore skirts and blouses or dresses to school and the Oliver trio learned the art of folding up their skirts carefully around them under the slacks which they wore en route so that they would appear in school neat and uncreased.

Despite the fact that Bill was away from home so much and when on the ranch commuted to Calgary daily, the family participated actively in the life of the community. They joined Christ Church, Millarville, the historic Anglican church built of upright logs which remains a famed feature of the district. At times Bill was chosen as the church's delegate to the Anglican Synod in Calgary. His wife Marjorie joined the Guild, an active ladies' church organization, the girls became members of the Anglican Young People's Association while Joan often played the organ for the church services. Bill and Marjorie Oliver attended bridge parties and took part in general community activities. During several winter seasons amateur theatre was a part of the Millarville scene; the plays produced helped with financial support for the church in addition to affording entertainment, fun and a measure of sustained effort for participants. The Oliver home often provided a rehearsal centre. Indeed, the Olivers were most hospitable and frequently invited neighbours for parties or entertained at delight-

Cattle in holding pens after roundup in southern Alberta, ca.1920s

ful evenings of film showings. They enjoyed having guests in their home. Their circle of friends was wide including a broad scope of interesting people with whom Bill had worked and many he had met on his travels across the country. A typical picture of an evening at Olivers reveals Bill, a genial host and an excellent raconteur, standing in characteristic pose with his back to the fireplace, his pipe in his hand, recounting to a fascinated group of listeners the story of some exciting experience; also the scene shows Marjorie, a charming hostess, moving among her guests assuring their ease and comfort.

Bill and Marjorie Oliver enjoyed their home and the freedom and appeal of living in the country. Nevertheless the move meant a great deal of extra work for each of them. When Bill returned from a trip he lost no time in plunging into the work on the place, driven it seemed by an apparently inexhaustible store of energy, and his interest in the Diamond L. He would check with his foreman regarding developments and problems, and soon would be involved in fencing, building corrals, branding, riding out to look at the cattle or others of the dozens of jobs required on a ranch. Then there were management decisions and activities, such as the purchase of animals, the culling of cattle, selection of feeders to retain, feeding programs to establish, beef to ship. Also, he kept careful stock feed and general records and the ranch books were his responsibility. In addition, true to his profession as a photographer, he took pictures and film footage of the animals and general ranch activities. From the latter he produced a film of binding, stooking and threshing which he sold to a grain company.

During the middle 1930s, the years when Bill Oliver was starting to build up his ranch, he remained deeply involved with Parks Branch assignments and so continued to be absent from home a great deal. For example, in 1935 his schedule was as follows: 26-27 January—Banff; 27 January - 13 February—home; 14-19 February—Vancouver; 20 February—Kamloops; 21 February - 5 March—home; 6-23 March—Banff, Sunshine, for ski story; 23 March - 10 April—home; 11 April—Calgary, photographing Lord and Lady Bessborough; 15 April—Calgary, showing film at CPR function; 17-18 April—Banff, photographing Lord and Lady Baden Powell and other dignitaries; 18-19 April—home; 20-23 April—Banff, photographing New Zealand Premier, Australian school boys and others; 23 April - 22 May—home; 23 May - 2 June—Kamloops and area fishing film; 22 June - 2 July—home; 3-24 July—Regina, Prince Albert, Lake Waskesiu, filming Grey Owl and beavers; 3-12 August—Victoria, Alberni, filming; 12 August - 1 September—home; 2-14 September—Regina, Prince Albert, Lake Waskesiu, continuing Grey Owl filming; 14-29 September—home; 30 September - 7 October—Victoria, Campbell River, filming salmon fishing; 7 October - 29 November—home; 30 November - 6 December—Wild Horse, Manyberries, Foremost and Lethbridge, filming antelope; 6-31 December—home.[4]

Between Bill's trips he commuted daily to his studio in Calgary, a round trip of some sixty-four miles, regardless of weather and roads. Highway 22 running south of Priddis to Turner Valley was gravelled in 1933-34,[5] improving transportation immensely, but there remained close to two miles of dirt road from his house to the closest point on the highway. There were times during the spring thaw or periods of heavy rain when the road became a morass of sticky mud, or in winter when the north-west wind piled the snow in great packed drifts. On such occasions, despite great effort on the driver's part and that of the car he drove, he was unable to shovel or churn his way through. Then one of the men from the ranch would come with a team to haul the car through the worst of the mud or snow.

While travelling, Bill kept as close contact as possible with his family. He wrote regularly to Marjorie and also kept up a steady flow of letters or post cards to the girls individually. In these he described interesting happenings relating to his photographic work, always writing in a vein which made each girl's letter a personal missive. He also remembered to gather items for the girls' collections. Writing to Joan from the *SS Normandie* in December 1937 he said, "A few more stamps for the collection—tell Spike [Doreen] have got coins for her but cannot mail them—also tell A.J. have not seen any rocks or leaves yet on this ocean trip . . . hope Mother never decides to collect china or old iron otherwise I shall have to get a few more trunks."[6]

Certainly the Oliver family was a happy one in which the bonds of love and mutual respect between all members were strong. Just to what extent the ranch acted as a unifying factor in the promotion of this spirit would be difficult to determine but to the girls their memorable growing up years on the Diamond L were enriching and rewarding.[7]

ON SAFARIS

By 1936 things were going well for Bill Oliver. There was no cessation of Parks Branch work and he knew he was fortunate, professionally and financially, to have the opportunity of carrying out these assignments. Then came the crowning touch of his photographic career: the invitation to act as official photographer on the Lerners' big game hunting expedition to Africa. It was a challenge; it was also an honour as Michael Lerner undoubtedly could have had his choice of photographers on the continent.

Accustomed as they were to excitement, the feelings of the Oliver family reached a new peak during the October days of 1936. On 3 November they boarded the Calgary to Montreal train, Marjorie and the girls bound for England and Bill for New York, then Africa. As planned, Bill saw his family comfortably aboard the *Duchess of Richmond* on 6 November and watched her steam off down the St. Lawrence River.

Next day he arrived in New York where he spent a week in a flurry of activity. Finally, the expedition boarded the *S.S. Rex* where W.J. immediately assumed his official photographer's role and took moving pictures of the Lerners embarking and visiting with the relatives and friends who came to see them off. After a rough five-day journey, the ship sailed through the Straits of Gibraltar and arrived at Naples on 21 November. From there they travelled to Rome where they remained for three fully packed days.[8] Bill was interested in observing the people and in a letter written later to a Calgary friend he noted that there was a feeling of unease and fear in Italy. Tourists were advised that if they spoke negatively of Mussolini it would be well to do so anonymously. Travellers like Bill Oliver who carried British passports were thoroughly scrutinized and as he was a photographer they searched him and his equipment with particular care, sealing his cameras before the party could leave for Athens.[9]

After a very bumpy aeroplane flight over the Mediterranean the party arrived at Alexandria, then entrained for Cairo where three days were spent in sightseeing, and, on Bill's part, photographing, with special emphasis on the daily life of the people. On the flight south the plane landed at Luxor for breakfast, Wadi Halfa for lunch, where the temperature was 93°F., then across the Nubian Desert to Kareina for tea, and finally arriving at Khartoum where they had dinner and stayed the night. On the following day there were further stops for meals and Bill caught his first sight of herds of elephants, giraffes, and hippos, and took his first movie footage as the pilot obligingly brought the plane down within four hundred feet of the elephant herd. That night was spent at Juba, then after flying over a maze of native villages, farms and game trails along the banks of the Nile and a part of Lake Victoria, they eventually reached their immediate destination, Nairobi, Kenya.

Michael Lerner, head of the expedition, was a field associate of the American Museum of Natural History and well versed in big game hunting procedures. A rather large man, he had the authoritative air of one who was accustomed to having his own way. His wife Helen, some years younger than he, was small, dark and vivacious; she could discuss the merits of various rifles and the techniques of shooting with any group of hunters and, like her husband, was an excellent shot.[10] As might be expected with his experience and wealth, Lerner had secured the services of one of Africa's most noted professional guides and hunters, Philip Percival. Bill was surprised to find that the man was a relative of Fred Percival, Earl of Egmont, a well known character in the Calgary area whom he had frequently photographed. In the afternoon Bill with his camera accompanied Percival to his farm at Machakos, some forty miles south-east of Nairobi. The weather was very pleasant and the beautiful countryside, treed and hilly, was reminiscent in the photographer's eyes of the Millarville area, except for the giraffe and gazelle along the way. He stayed the night in the Percival's lovely home and then was taken on an overnight camera trip to the Southern Game Reserve. They camped near a waterhole and he was able to photograph giraffe, zebra, kongoni, and impalla. The following day they returned to the farm where the natives staged a dance, rather mysterious and awesome to western eyes. Bill filmed the proceedings.

On 9 December the safari left Nairobi. It consisted of Michael

Bill Oliver, taking ranching view, ca.1920s

and Helen Lerner, Bill Oliver, guide Philip Percival, his assistant Ben Fourie, and an army of porters and other natives ready to serve every need of the hunters and cameraman. They travelled north in an assortment of cars and trucks loaded with hunting, camera, and camping equipment. Several days were spent around the slopes of Mount Kenya and during that time the Lerners obtained several trophies, mainly kongoni and oryx. At Isiolo they crossed into the Northern Frontier of Kenya where they met Major Remington, District Commissioner in command of a force of native police. When Lerner referred to his photographer as "Canada," which he often did, the commissioner wanted to know the part of Canada Oliver was from, on being told, "Out West," he showed particular interest. It transpired that he had been with the Royal North-West Mounted Police at Medicine Hat and knew Alberta well.

The safari continued north, finding herds of zebra and gazelle of different kinds, bands of chattering baboons, many giraffe and some rhino, ostrich and elephant. Bill was amazed at the way in which vultures by the dozens appeared out of nowhere immediately a kill was made and he found much to photograph. The plan had been to hunt elephant in Abyssinia (Ethiopia) but it was discovered that the country was still in a state of unrest following the Italian conquest in May of that year. Groups of prisoners of war were in stockades and stragglers from Haile Selassie's defeated army still roamed the country. Another deterrent was the poor condition of roads. It was decided instead to return to Nairobi and then continue south into Tanganyika. During the latter part of the trip south, they encountered heavy rains and the trucks constantly got bogged down in mudholes, having to be jacked up, brush put under the wheels, and sometimes unloaded before being pushed out. It was heavy work but the natives' efforts ultimately met with success. At times the skies cleared and the sun shone forth with blazing heat; on occasions there was morning sun and then the party was treated to views of Mount Kilimanjaro, magnificent with its glaciers and snow capped peaks. In the ancient city of Mombasa, Bill was fascinated with the narrow streets, colourful bazaars, diverse peoples, heavily veiled women, and natives with great loads of wares. The whole safari then assembled at Voi, with plans to embark on a foray into elephant country the next day. There was a feeling

African safari, 1936

Michael Lerner with bubal on African safari, 1936

Unloading safari trucks at campsite, 1936

Removing trophy tusks from elephant during African safari, 1936

of excited anticipation about the forthcoming hunt but as the travellers sat around their campfire that evening their thoughts were of home; it was Christmas Eve and visions of past Christmases filled their minds.

With the dawning of Christmas Day spirits rose. Good wishes were exchanged and in short order all was packed and the safari on its way to the elephant hunting camp. Percival's native trackers had scouted the area and had good reports of elephants so expectations were high. The weather was showery and roads bad but these conditions did not detract from the cheerful mood. The campsite was reached about noon and, as elephants were reported to be about five miles away, Lerner with guide, gun bearers and trackers set out on a hunt shortly after lunch. Bill went to his tent to clean his cameras and check film and when he emerged he found that Mrs. Lerner, who had also remained in camp, had decorated the dining tent for Christmas. Here in the heart of the jungle appeared a dining room glowing with tinsel, holly, crackers, party favours and all the traditional trappings of a western Christmas dinner. It was a heartwarming surprise.

The hunters, who soon appeared wet, tired, and without trophies, also were delighted. They dressed for dinner, but when about to sit down a storm hit with thunder, lightning, and deluge of rain. The camp was awash in a few minutes with rain blowing into the dining tent and spoiling the decorations. As usual the natives came to the rescue and by using an extra tarp excluded most of the driving rain. The Lerners played the part of Santa Claus and produced gifts for the whole group including all the natives. Eventually the party sat down to a real Christmas dinner—fish, hot roast duck, cold boiled beef, Christmas pudding alight with brandy, nuts, raisins, chocolates, and, of course, liquid refreshments. They agreed that their cook had done a marvellous job, despite the pelting rain. The dinner was wonderful and the fact that they sat with their feet in puddles of water was unimportant. They all rose and drank the health of the family of each and of absent friends. It was a jovial party but at 9:30 they retired, still to the accompaniment of driving rain.

Two days later, Lerner shot the type of elephant he sought. Indeed, this one was truly a patriarch, estimated to be well over a hundred years old; he was immense, weighing approximately five tons and measuring eleven feet, two inches from tail to withers. His tusks, the trophy part of an elephant, also were huge and weighed 100 and 107 pounds respectively. Bill was moved by the sight of the fallen monarch, but he was there as a photographer so he took a series of pictures of the proud hunter beside his great catch. The natives then started their work. They had a difficult time extracting the tusks which were deeply imbedded in the bone, and in removing the one and a half inch thick hide. They had barely completed the job when a band of native men, women, and children from a village in the vicinity arrived to get the meat. They built rough drying racks and as the men carved off the strips of meat the women and children carried them to the rack. There was a great feast that night and an abundance of food for days to come.

The safari gradually moved northward, and the Lerners continued collecting trophies. They ascended to the top of the Ngorongoro Crater over a dirt road which was well engineered and very scenic. The view from the top was most spectacular. The country west of the crater was mainly bamboo jungle and a good area for rhinos. Shortly a fine rhino was secured and the party then moved on to the Serengeti Plain in northern Tanganyika. En route Bill obtained some good photographs of lions and then came an opportunity for an amazing and unusual wildlife movie. They were driving slowly along when they espied a lioness and her two full grown cubs stalking an unsuspecting zebra. Ben Fourie edged the car into position for photographing and Bill was able to film the whole hunt. The lioness crouched low in the grass and every time the zebra lowered its head to graze she stealthily gained yards on her prey, while the cubs at her heels followed her every move. Suddenly they all rushed forward, two of them springing onto the zebra's back and the other going towards its head. It managed to buck off one of the lions but shortly was brought to the ground. When the male cub had the zebra by the throat and the female a grip on the groin the lioness left them to finish the job and wandered off. They had received a lesson in hunting and capturing their food; it was the law of the jungle by which they would live. While the lions were wrestling their victim to the ground, Bill had the car brought in closer to the scene until he was filming from a distance of fifty feet. Lerner on one side and Percival on the other covered him with their high powered rifles but the lions were so interested in capturing and devouring their prey that they seemed oblivious to the presence of people or car. The following day when out hunting, the men drove past the site of the kill and they saw the lioness still lying beside the half-eaten carcass, keeping away a dozen or so hyenas and jackals and scores of vultures. The two cubs lay stretched in the shade of a nearby tree replete and satisfied.

Bill Oliver saw the Serengeti Plain as a lovely area, some of it park-like in nature. He marvelled at the numbers and varieties of game animals; from the eminence of Lion Hill, for example, as they observed the countryside through field glasses, there seemed to be a seething mass of life in all directions. He took movie footage of huge herds of gazelle, zebra and wildebeest, of cheetahs making a kill, of lions which on one occasion circled the car at dangerously close range, of leopards, water buffalo, and rhinos. He also filmed Helen Lerner stalking and bagging a rhino and a lion. Animals came close to camp and as the party sat around the fire in the evening they could hear lions roaring, jackals barking and the weird indescribable noise of hyenas. Often throughout the night the sound continued; on one occasion the lions made a kill a mere two hundred yards from camp and the night reverberated with the noise. In this area there were game restrictions to observe; for example, one lion only per hunter was permitted, and there were quotas on certain other animals such as cheetahs.

The safari remained on the plain for eighteen days, then on 1 February 1937, they left, rather reluctantly, but the weather had become increasingly wet and when rains were really heavy it was impossible to get in or out of the plains area. After a hard morning's climb they reached the Ngorongoro Crater and had lunch on its rim where they could look back at Serengeti. They then travelled southward to the Mthumbu River country, the Lerners completing their game quotas and Bill photographing when possible.

His movie making was not restricted to the hunt and wildlife alone but also reflected his interest in the native peoples. He made movies of the bearers carrying out their work around the camp, a procedure in which they were delighted to co-operate. He visited the villages and learned about the customs and practices of the different tribes in the country through which he passed and when possible filmed them. At one village he was permitted to photograph a religious dance and circumcision ceremony performed by the Mokoma tribe. It was believed to be the first time that photographing of this ceremony had been allowed.

On 6 February, the safari divided. The Lerners, scheduled soon to leave Africa, continued south to Nairobi with Percival, Fourie and most of the natives, while W.J. embarked on another safari which would be devoted entirely to picture taking. The group had lived and camped in close quarters for some two months, sharing unusual experiences which at times were difficult, or tedious, sometimes dangerous and at others thrilling, so parting was not without feeling. Bill, experienced trail camper that he was, rated Percival and Fourie high as hunting gentlemen and sportsmen. He felt great appreciation of the capabilities, integrity, and unfailing good nature of the natives. Their dependability impressed him particularly; for example, the gun-bearers during the tenseness of the hunt were fearless and seemed to sense and immediately fill the hunters' every need. The natives gave the white men names which signified something of their assessment of these people they served. Bill Oliver had two names, *Kapo*, meaning "always aiming" (with camera) and *Dak-tari*, meaning "kind and fair" to the natives. As a mark of respect they put on the photographer's wrists, bands made from the hair of an elephant's tail and tied in such a way that no ends of the hair were exposed. One of these bands became caught on something and tore loose but the other he wore for a considerable time.[11] Such bands were considered a good luck talisman.

For W.J.'s camera hunting safari his guide was George DeBeer, a young Dutchman who had a farm in the Arusha district and also specialized in capturing wild animals for sale to animal farms and zoos. With him came Andrea, his native guide or scout, and a number of other porters and helpers, while Molo, Bill's personal servant, Ndetta, his porter, and Meru, a cook, remained with him from the Lerner party. There followed days of arduous jungle travel, painstaking stalking and hours of patient waiting. There were times of tense expectation when animals appeared within the range of the camera lens, wondrous moments when they simply posed or acted with unconcerned detachment, or exceedingly anxious

Native guides skinning elephant foot, 1936

ones when they suddenly grew suspicious or angry and approached dangerously close to the blind. But perhaps Bill's most gratifying, although potentially dangerous, undertaking of this trip was the making of a movie of an elephant herd.

The country was dense jungle but DeBeer and Andrea knew the signs and after miles of travel brought Oliver to a group of feeding elephants. It was difficult to anticipate the direction they would travel and consequently where to set up the camera. Eventually the men determined the course they seemed to be taking and all was made ready. Andrea constantly tested the wind direction and velocity as it was essential that they prevent the elephants getting the scent of humans. In a few minutes some animals came within camera range. Then DeBeer whispered that he had located a second herd immediately behind the one they had stalked. They waited anxiously to see what action the second herd would take. Soon there appeared a grand parade of elephant cows, calves, and bulls passing across the field in view of the cameras. Occasionally a group would stop and apparently listen for sounds, although they themselves produced constant noise with great stomachs growling and huge ears constantly chafing against necks as they flapped to discourage flies. Suddenly from the dense bush behind the camera position came loud trumpeting and crashing trees; apparently another part of the herd was moving in. The men jumped up, grabbed the equipment and ran; it was close timing because within ten minutes a great company of elephants, the third part of the herd, passed directly over the place where they had been concealed. It was a frightening and exhausting experience but in the camera Bill clutched in his hands was a roll of marvellous film footage.

They next embarked on a hippo hunt but although days were spent in tracking, crossing swampy muskegs and skirting marshy pools they had no luck. At times they heard the animals grunting and splashing in the distance but were unable to stalk within filming distance and the wily animals avoided their well camouflaged camera set up. Monkeys screamed from the trees nearby, hordes of flies descended upon them, and mosquitoes, a constant malaria threat, buzzed about them. They waited until evening and then admitted defeat. Bill was philosophical about it, feeling that wildlife photography involves waiting, indefinite waiting, for breaks which might not come, but when they did all the effort, the waiting and the discomfort made the prize the more valuable and rewarding.

Despite the difficulties and frustrations of wildlife photography, this was the type of hunting which he enjoyed. He could appreciate good marksmanship with a rifle but he found camera shooting which left animals alive and free much more gratifying; the hunt was more difficult but infinitely more rewarding.

Eventually Bill Oliver had to give up his hippo quest as the time of his departure from Africa was near. Despite this disappointment he had cause for satisfaction. He had shot 38,000 feet of motion picture film, some of which was in colour, besides a broad representation of still photographs and a number of slide series. The safari arrived back in Nairobi on 21 February, where he said good-bye to DeBeer and his native crew and left for England.

Meanwhile his family was awaiting his arrival with eager anticipation. Marjorie and his brother Reg met him in London and the girls could hardly contain their excitement until his train reached Ash the following day. Despite regular correspondence during the past months the reunited family had much to talk about. There were details of Bill's adventures to hear and for them, there had been the new experience of life in a tranquil English village.

After Bill's return the family remained in England for over a month. There were various excursions during this time including a trip to London where the photographer had a number of commitments resulting from the fame he had achieved as a wildlife photographer and through his African adventure. This included an interview by the British Broadcasting Corporation. The girls were delighted to see their father's photographs hanging in Canada House, London, the office of Canadian Steamship Lines, and in various hotels. None of these works bore his name but they were very familiar to the family. Furthermore, on their return trip the entertainment included an Oliver film, "She Climbs to Conquer."

Back in Alberta, Bill undertook a number of speaking engagements, some Parks Branch assignments, and then at the beginning of September came another big game hunting expedition with the Lerners. This had resulted from some of Bill's own stories told around African jungle campfires when he

Helen Lerner with zebra on 1936 African safari

talked of wild animals in western Canada, of grizzlies, caribou, and elk, sure-footed mountain goats, and the rare and seldom seen blue sheep, the Ovis Stonei. It was this last bit of information that especially triggered the hunters' attention. They decided that they must discover these elusive animals, and while in the region they would bag other specimens from the mountain regions of the Canadian West. Some of these would make welcome additions to the American Museum of Natural History. Acting for Lerner, Bill obtained the services of Jack Brewster as guide and outfitter and made other necessary arrangements.

On 30 August 1937, the Lerners arrived at the CNR station in Edmonton. Bill had wanted them to meet his family and especially to give his family the opportunity of viewing the African films. Lerner arranged a private showing for a small group of people at the MacDonald Hotel, of what he considered to be "the finest photographs of wild animal life that had ever come out of the dark continent."[12] It was a three-hour showing and Helen Fraser, one privileged viewer, writing in the *Calgary Herald* described the movies enthusiastically. She was obviously thrilled by the myriads of wild animals, the African veldt, and the jungle where they lived.[13] Helen Lerner proclaimed that this material, which was her property, was "too precious" and meant too much to her to release for commercial use.[14] This attitude, which precluded public viewing, evoked some criticism in the press.[15]

The Lerners and W.J. flew from Edmonton to Trimble Lake in northern B.C. to the camp which Brewster had already established. The lake lies in the remote country between Great Snow Mountain and Mount Trimble and from there the party penetrated even more deeply into the mountain vastness.[16] Game abounded and within a few days each of the Lerners had bagged a blue sheep, Helen's being the larger and the world's record trophy for a woman.[17]

Flying from there to Jasper, the Lerners left on the second lap of their hunt. Brewster had his pack pony outfit ready and with Jasper guide, Dorrel Shovar assisting, they set out for the game country north of Jasper National Park. Here the names of places where they camped and hunted had for Bill a familiar ring—Willow Creek, Sholl Banks, Rock Creek, Summit, Goat Mountain, Eagle Nest Pass. The Lerners shot caribou, moose, Big Horn sheep, mountain goats, and grizzly. Again W.J. in addition to filming the hunters downing their prey and the trophies they obtained, went on his own camera hunting forays. As usual some days of waiting brought only emptiness and others were starred with good luck and success. His most gratifying catch on the trip was some excellent footage of moose engaging in their daily routine of life.

The trip ended on 18 October. Bill returned home and spent the next ten days editing the film. This was demanding, meticulous work. Although an energetic outdoors man whose broad hands and fingers bespoke hard physical work he could handle and splice small pieces of film with dexterity and infinite care and patience. Eventually the Jasper movie was completed and mailed to the Lerners in New York.

Before Christmas 1937, Bill Oliver was in New York and ready to join another Lerner expedition. They sailed on the *S.S. Normandie* for England, went on to Amsterdam, then across Europe to India where they spent some seventeen days travelling by train and motor car to such places as Jodhpur,

Jaipur, Delhi, Agra, Benares, and Calcutta. Included in their tour were excursions to numerous notable sights, one of the most impressive being the Taj Mahal. They then travelled through Burma and Siam before coming to French Indo-China where an extensive hunting expedition was scheduled. Here they motored to Pnom Penh and then on to Saigon in Cochin, China where they were met by their guide and outfitter, a Frenchman, A. Plas. The party went by truck to Djiring in the north-west part of the Province of Annam where their main objective was hunting tiger.[18] From Djiring travel was by foot through rough country covered by dense steaming jungle.

When tiger tracks were discovered, the natives of the party —the Mois from the remote mountainous regions—built a *boma* to conceal either hunter or cameraman. This structure, shaped like a beehive, was made out of bamboo thatched with a jungle grass, with a hole cut just large enough for a camera lens and another as a peephole. The *boma* was wonderfully concealed in jungle growth; bait in the form of the carcass of a young buffalo was staked out some thirty-five feet away. Bill spent several days waiting. The heat was intense, flies and mosquitoes buzzed constantly, small lizards came to visit, crickets in the surrounding trees chorused continually, and when the breeze blew from the bait towards the shelter the smell of the rapidly decaying carcass was almost unbearable. At times he heard elephants, Gibbon apes, and various other animals. A huge dragon lizard fed for awhile on the bait, then a boar appeared and while it was dining a wild cock and three hens strutted into the camera's view range. All of them were recorded. Suddenly they took flight and left and presently the tense watcher saw grasses moving as some animal stealthily approached. It was not the tiger he had been expecting but a huge cat, a golden panther. It was one of the rarest species in Indo-China and the excellent pictures obtained of it devouring the bait was an unexpected bonus.[19] Time was spent, too, in another type of blind, a *mirador*, which was raised some ten feet off the ground and provided a good view of the surrounding country.

Although tigers had avoided the photographer's blinds they abounded in the area. A native policeman was killed by one about two miles from the expedition's camp. Later both the Lerners had the opportunity for shots and each bagged a tiger. Bill meanwhile was putting his camera to good use in photographing wild boar, lizards, and various other animals. He also made movies of the Mois people, their village life, dances, and ceremonies.[20]

For part of the hunt the party travelled to the northern town of Ban-me-Thuot, which was the headquarters of the French government in that part of Annam. Here they were entertained at the residency and then taken to visit a Moi chief's home. Later the resident, Monsieur Salamon, escorted them by car a distance of some eighty miles to the village of Boum-Ma-Moi, the most northerly French outpost, where a French officer and some 300 soldiers were stationed in a fortified post. The Mois in this area were resentful of French authority and there was always danger of attack by marauding bands. Here the party was supplied with elephants for travel and a still larger escort accompanied them on the hunt. Bill's steed was a bit obstreperous but an elephant rider perched on the animal's head managed to make him obey. He made friends with this native who had been assigned to him and although neither knew anything of the other's language, they got along very well. The young man was keenly interested in the camera and obviously found looking through the viewfinder an amazing experience. Bill shared cigarettes with him and when leaving gave him a box of matches, a present which delighted the natives and was especially welcome because for the most part these people used steel and flint to produce fire.[21]

In this region the game consisted mainly of gaur—a type of massive wild ox—elephant and buffalo; the latter were numerous and could be very dangerous. Bill narrowly missed collision with one. He was standing at his camera tripod photographing one animal and didn't see another buffalo that suddenly appeared on the other side and charged. One of the natives saw the danger, grabbed Bill around the legs and carried him out of the buffalo's path. In the commotion the charging animal swerved slightly and missed smashing the camera; the photographer was almost as thankful for the camera's survival as he was for his own. The native who rescued him was slight of build but very strong and quick in action, which was indeed fortunate as this was a danger which might well have ended in disaster.[22]

The party left Phnom Penh and on 16 April flew to Alex-

Michael Lerner in Moi village, Indo-China, 1938

andria and entrained for Cairo. Bill Oliver parted from the Lerners here and continued south by plane to Beira, Mozambique, where he met Philip Percival who again was to act as guide. The main purpose of this trip was to obtain further buffalo, lion, and elephant pictures. They hunted mainly in the Zambesi River area where the weather was intensely hot; on many days there would be a fifteen or twenty mile walk through swamps and tall grass but the reward was some wonderful buffalo pictures. Good water buck and zebra films also were obtained and more footage taken of the dances and ceremonies of native peoples. On this occasion, Bill Oliver developed malaria and he was in bed for two days enduring the extreme chills and high fever that typify the disease. The quinine which the travellers carried helped in its control and soon he was up and travelling although not fully reçovered.[23]

Bill carried on with his camera hunting until the end of May. He felt Africa to be a marvellous country despite the heat, the glaring brilliance of the sun with its burning intensity that affected skin and eyes, and despite its disease-bearing insects.[24] He found the prolific animal life and the excellent photographic possibilities exciting. The animals' great size and ferocity and the potential danger in filming them did not bother him; indeed he often said that for fierceness the grizzly bear of the western Canadian mountains overshadowed even the lion, the king of the beasts. But Africa left her mark upon him—the malaria which reoccurred periodically during the years that followed.

Bill Oliver left Beira on 9 June, and on his return to Alberta he spent some two weeks editing the Indo-China and African films. The Lerners came to Edmonton to view these in early October and again were delighted with the results.

Life returned to normal for W.J. then. This included frequent trips around the country carrying out commissions for the Parks Branch, some studio work including photographing celebrities in Calgary, Banff, and Edmonton, fulfilling speaking engagements, and spending time whenever possible at the ranch. The Oliver family had developed a pattern of living whereby they moved to the ranch at the beginning of summer holidays and spent the school year in the city. Christmas and most other holidays as well as many weekends, saw the family back on the Diamond L.

It transpired that the Lerners' trip to the mountains of northern B.C. and Alberta had whetted their appetite for hunting in the north-west. They were particularly anxious to secure Kodiak bear found only in the extreme north. In August 1939, W.J. met the couple again, this time in Seattle where they took a cruise ship to Steward, Alaska. From here the party, nine in number including Lerner's nephew Bill, flew to Anchorage, took the train to Fairbanks, then proceeded by car on a new highway to Circle Springs, a hot springs resort, where they enjoyed a short stop before continuing to Circle City. At Porcupine River they saw countless numbers of cari-

A. J. and Doreen Oliver at Sinclair Canyon, Kootenay National Park, 1941

bou in migration, a marvellous photographic opportunity. Then in the Wood River country they hunted the rare Dall Sheep which are similar to the Rocky Mountain variety but pure white. Here hunters with guns and cameras both were successful.

At that point a heavy snow storm prevented travel for six days. The guides had secured some pack horses from Mount McKinley Park but the men had a difficult time getting the animals out. While there, the Lerners bagged a moose and grizzlies. As always Bill secured good animal film footage, although at one point when the going was very bad, his film was dumped into the river and he had to send to Anchorage for more. Later the party flew to the Tustumena Lake area on the Kenai Peninsula where they found more Dall sheep, moose, and black bear. At last they had had to give up the quest for Kodiak bear because the weather had turned so cold that seaplanes were unable to take them to Kodiak Island. By now the temperature was consistently low so they headed homeward on the *S.S. Alaska* docking at Seattle in late October.

In an interview for the *Albertan* Bill Oliver said that he much preferred the cold of the Arctic to Africa's heat. Furthermore, he declared, "breathing the frosty air is a recognized cure for malaria victims."[25] At one time, before the mosquito was recognized as the malaria culprit, it was believed that the disease was contracted by breathing the hot, humid air of the tropics; conversely it could be assumed that cold, frosty air would have a salutary effect. Possibly Bill had this in mind when making his statement, but likely there was a twinkle in his eye at the time.

On 4 September 1939, while in Alaska, Bill heard the news of the outbreak of war. This was not unexpected as on his trips through Europe he had seen signs of the coming turmoil and in Britain he had been aware of preparation for this eventuality. He still had deep feelings for his homeland and there was the added concern about his mother, brother, and other relatives living there. He voiced something of these worries in a letter to Joan written on her birthday, 2 October. He wrote feelingly, too, of Poland's plight and spoke of the troubled times in England.[26] He could not suspect the extent of the coming conflagration nor the fact that the lives of people in most parts of the world, his own included, would be affected.

Feeder cattle in corral at Diamond L Ranch. ca.1930s

Pack outfit in the high country, ca.1930s

VI. Rustle of Aspen Leaves

With the commencement of the 1940s, W. J. Oliver started winding down his photographic career. In the aspect of photography which was his forte—filming animal life—his accomplishments were truly impressive. With his camera he had captured most of the animals native to Canada, with the possible exception of the otter and the Polar bear.[1] Also, myriads of birds had appeared in his works. His African filming safaris had resulted in movies showing a wide variety of wildlife which were amazing in their portrayal of animal customs and life. He was considered by many experts to be "the leading wildlife photographer of North America."[2] No man could reasonably expect to do more.

Bill Oliver's withdrawal from photographic work was a gradual process. Although he carried out fewer assignments for the Parks Branch—mainly because of the effects the war was producing on the branch's undertakings—he did continue to submit movies to Ottawa at least as late as 1941. Also, Michael Lerner remained in touch with him and made periodic requests for his photographic services.

When the Lerners were anxious to return to Alaska for further hunting, Bill joined them in Seattle in the summer of 1940 and again they sailed northward. The Lerners obtained sheep, caribou, grizzly and black bear trophies, while Bill was able to make some good movies of moose, sheep and caribou. He was back home on the ranch by mid-October and soon busily engaged with threshing. Another Lerner swordfishing expedition which saw Bill Oliver on hand was scheduled for the summer of 1946 but because of fog and high seas the undertaking was unsuccessful. Bill, however, enjoyed seeing old friends as well as rephotographing Louisbourg and other familiar haunts.[3] That same year saw his last trip to Africa. In the fall he left Calgary, spent over a week in New York, then departed by plane with the Lerners for Kenya. After a leisurely trip with various stops en route, they arrived at Nairobi where they were again met by Philip Percival.[4] The Lerners on this expedition proposed getting trophies and also African native weapons and other artifacts for the Nova Scotia Museum in Halifax. In fact it was advertised as the "Lerner African Expedition of the Nova Scotia Museum."[5] W.J. hoped to make further movies of animals in their natural habitat, focusing especially on lions and elephants, but he would be alert for any wildlife he could capture on film.

The safari was large. Two station wagons, two three-ton trucks, and a one-ton powerwagon pulled out of Nairobi. The party included four professional hunters and guides—Philip Percival, Pat Ayre who had taken the Duke and Duchess of York on a hunt, Captain Murray-Smith and Frank Bowman. In addition there were thirty-two native porters and eight personal native attendants. They headed northward finding no dearth of game and the veteran photographer had some thrilling as well as dangerous experiences. One involved a large buffalo bull. The animal was grazing and moving towards the camera set-up but when about a hundred feet away it became aware of the intrusion. He was very curious and after some hesitation advanced to investigate; when at about a distance of sixty feet he stopped, raising his head high and showing a great interest in the unusual object. Bill's camera whirred. To one side, concealed behind an uprooted mimosa tree and watching the buffalo's every movement were Michael Lerner and Frank Bowman with guns in readiness. The buffalo decided to investigate further and came on at a trot headed straight for the camera. When he was about forty feet away the hunters decided that he was as close as safety permitted and a shot ended his progress. The movie showing the aroused buffalo advancing steadily closer to the viewer was really spectacular.

Another film which proved delightful was of a herd of some seventy elephant cows and calves. They were feeding, then drinking and bathing in a small river. The calves, some very young and less than three feet high, played and gambolled, spraying water over each other and running to their mothers. The weather this day was excessively hot, around 125° Fahrenheit or higher, and very humid. Bill and his guide who were without water, longed for a drink of that which the elephants were squandering. It was an exhausting three-hour hunt but Bill felt the result was worth the effort. When the party reached

Isiolo, the entrance to the Northern Frontier which is the gateway to Ethiopia, they noted a big difference from the time of their 1937 visit. Then there were no roads but now a military highway stretched from Isolo to Addis Ababa in Ethiopia. There also was evidence of bombing around the Isiolo area.

Bill Oliver returned to Canada in February 1947, and was precipitated into a period of very cold weather and deep snow. Just weeks after leaving Africa's sweltering jungle he was stuck in snow drifts on the road to his Millarville ranch but he still claimed he preferred the snow to the heat.[6]

During the years before his 1946-47 African safari, W.J. made some momentous changes in the pattern of his life. In 1941, he moved to the ranch on a more permanent basis, ending his daily commuting to Calgary and freeing the major part of his time for ranch management and work. This meant sharp curtailment of involvement with his studio and picture taking activities generally. Then on 1 April 1942, he sold the studio business to Walter Cadman who since 1927 had been second in command. Although he relinquished his interest in the enterprise at this time the Oliver name was retained with the studio for another thirty years.

Besides the natural phasing down of his activities in the photographic field he was probably motivated in this decision by two factors. One was his desire to expand and improve his ranch operation and the other grew out of his strong feelings of patriotism, for now the nation had an urgent need for farm and ranch produce. Furthermore, as the war years advanced and more young men joined up, it became increasingly difficult to hire farm help. Meanwhile the quality of the cattle Bill Oliver was raising had become recognized. For example, the *Market Examiner*, Calgary, in 1945 noted: "Bill Oliver topping the market this week on his steers, shouldn't have to worry much about selling those whiteface bulls of his. Bill must have something—remember, he was at the top on some of his steers a year ago, too."[7] Again in 1948 the *Examiner* commented on the fact that Oliver beef shipments consistently commanded top prices.[8]

Despite his ranch work and some photographic activity Bill still found time to share his movies and picture-taking experiences. Particularly during the late 1930s and throughout the 1940s he was much in demand as a lecturer. Many of his addresses centred around the theme of hunting with a camera instead of a gun. He emphasized the greater satisfaction and thrills of the camera sport and the greater expertise required and thus made a plea for wildlife conservation which was designed to appeal to sportsmen. With the talks he gave to organizations, very often he showed pictures and these, too, illustrated the appeal of the wild. Some of the groups to which he spoke were the Calgary Board of Trade, Kiwanis Club, Women's Canadian Club, Alberta Military Institute, Knights of the Round Table, Rotary Club, Alpine Club, Knights of Columbus, and many church and school groups in southern Alberta.

In mid-summer of 1946, Bill Oliver made his last trip with Michael Lerner when again they went to Africa, not returning until the new year.

On the ranch, Bill found it increasingly difficult to find sufficient reliable hands; a swing away from the land appeared to be in progress and able-bodied young men were going into other lines of endeavour. He had worked hard on the ranch during the previous decade and possibly now felt that he should have more leisure and less demanding deffort. Also, his career had afforded constant change and motion and probably, consciously or unconsciously, he resented the restrictions and the routine that ranch work and management imposed; freedom and travel had been the keynotes of his life and he thrived on them. As a result, in the summer of 1949 he sold the Diamond L Ranch. He had put enthusiastic effort into the building of the place to the peak he desired and now that his dream was fulfilled there was no longer the challenge which spurred his interest. F. E. B. Gourley and Sons of Edinburgh, Scotland, were the purchasers. An auction sale of cattle, horses, farm machinery, and household furniture held on 26 October 1949, was reported enthusiastically in the *Calgary Herald*. Under the heading, "Oliver Ranch Auction Grosses Nearly $37,000," the reporter claimed that the crowd of 3,500 in attendance was the largest of any farm sale held in Alberta.[9]

The Olivers' move to town, to the Belvedere Apartments, occurred in the fall of 1949. The people of the Millarville district were sincerely sorry to see them leave; they invited the family to a gathering at the Church House, a community hall near Christ Church, Millarville, for the presentation of a token of

Joan Oliver at the ranch, ca.1930s

appreciation to former good neighbours and the expression of good wishes for their future.

After the physical and emotional strain of their last days at the ranch Bill and Marjorie Oliver were very tired, however their days of resting in Calgary were few. In November Bill bought a new house at 602 Rideau Road and he plunged immediately into house renovations. Soon architects were involved in planning an addition which would provide a long room suitable for movie projection.

There were various other interests and activities in Bill Oliver's life during the next few years. He and Marjorie had many friends and as always enjoyed an active social life. One of their regular engagements was playing bridge in a club formed mainly of ex-Millarville people. And of course, there were some trips, periodic visits to the mountains, to California, and to England.

After 1952, although still relatively active, Bill Oliver undertook work with his collection of photographs and movies. He intended to get them fully identified and organized but did not make much progress with this task. He had had little time for picture identification when his life was packed with action for then his main interest had been in taking the pictures. Now, the sedentary, rather pedestrian job of turning back the pages of time and documenting these views did not appeal to him.

On 19 April 1954, Bill Oliver died in the General Hospital in Calgary after a very brief illness, his death resulting from internal bleeding from an aortic aneurism. Although he had not reached his sixty-seventh birthday, he had lived his life fully, literally accomplishing more than many men could in two or more lifetimes. He was a remarkable man. Modest and unassuming about his accomplishments, they were nevertheless important to him as a measure of worth and a source of satisfaction. Once in a letter to Joan he expressed something of his philosophy, saying, "... it is one of the greatest reflections in life (in my estimation) to be able to look back and be proud of something accomplished and well done."[10]

By nature he was determined and persistent; there was sincerity, kindliness and a puckish sense of humour in his approach to life; he had high standards in his relationships to which he adhered and he expected others to do the same. He was astute in business, an outdoorsman of boundless energy and vigourous activity, and at the same time he was an artist, acutely sensitive to beauty. As one writer said, "His medium is the camera; with it in his hands he is a gifted artist, with the artist's eye and sense of beauty and imaginative understanding."[11] Open and outgoing, he was completely at ease with people of all walks of life, making friends easily and attracting the regard of others. All of these were important to him, from his lawyer friends and colleagues on the *Herald* to the wranglers on the trail, from the native in Indo-China who in an expression of affection rubbed his forehead against his new friend's arm, to Sir Dennis and Lady Herbert, also met on his travels, who showed their esteem by entertaining him at dinner at the House of Commons in London.

W.J. Oliver's photographic work is a legacy that he has left to Canada. His pictures illustrating life of Canadians during the teens, twenties, and thirties, portraying ranch and farm activities, modes of transportation, views of towns and cities, people at work, in sports or at leisure, noted figures in public office—these in the perspective of time are historical documents, valuable for research now and for future generations. Also his scenic views, his wildlife stills and movies, because of their naturalness, the poetic treatment given them and their absolute sincerity, have an enduring quality. A current photographer speaks of photographs as fine art, emphasizing the difference in effect of "taking" a picture as opposed to, with an artist's eye, "making" a picture, which then communicates the union of the photographer's impressions with the reality of the subject matter.[12] This is something that Bill Oliver some forty years earlier was able to accomplish. The unchanging freshness and the universality of his works are indicated by awards won in October 1954, in a German Festival, "International Exhibition of Big Game Hunting and Fishing" in Dusseldorf, Germany. "Return of the Buffalo" received a gold medal and "Strange Doings in Beaver Land" was winner of a silver medal. Some twenty-three years later Parks Canada mounted an exhibition of Oliver photographs of the national parks which toured central Canada, the Maritimes, and the West as far as Banff. In 1977, the Public Affairs Department of Toronto Arts Production in co-operation with the Toronto Filmmakers Co-op, as a tribute to Canada's film pioneers presented a showing of a selection of their works. Included was Oliver's "Hunting without a Gun."

It has been said of Bill Oliver that the filming of his wildlife movies demanded "all the effort of the big game hunter, the endurance of the explorer, the courage of the RCMP, the patience of Job, and the kindness to animals of St. Francis of Assisi."[13] In actual fact greater effort than that of the big game hunter was required. Bill had felt that the hunter missed "the real thrill of the chase" and pointed out that the man with the camera must approach the animal much more closely, and thus in fact perform a greater feat of stalking.[14] Of the requirements for filming wild animals he himself stressed patience. However, perhaps the greatest underlying component of Bill Oliver's success with his scenic and wildlife pictures was his love of the things of nature and the great outdoors. Here was a man who out of the depth of his feeling for God's world and his desire to be close to it, planted aspen poplars outside his bedroom window so he could hear the rustle of the wind in their leaves at night.

View of Calgary, looking north-west, ca.1930s

Southern Alberta harvest, ca.1920s

List of Films

The following is a list of all known motion picture films taken by W. J. Oliver. Except for Fox News films, the date of production given is, generally speaking, the year following that of actual filming. Square brackets indicate films for which titles are not known. Abbreviations used are as follows: PB - Parks Branch; FN - Fox News; NFA - National Film Archives; NFB - National Film Board; PABC - Provincial Archives of B.C.

The list is compiled from data obtained from the following sources: the Oliver family, including the W. J. Oliver papers and a list of films donated to Canadian Film Archives by Mrs. W. J. Oliver in 1973; *Catalogue of Motion Picture Films*, National Parks Bureau, 1943; information from David Mattison, Sound and Moving Image Division, Provincial Archives of B.C. and P.A.B.C. film catalogue cards; information from Andris Kesteris, National Film Archives, and NFA catalogue cards; Colin Browne, *Motion Picture Production in British Columbia, 1898-1940* (Province of B.C., 1979); and Peter Morris, *Embattled Shadows: A History of Canadian Cinema, 1895-1939* (Montreal: McGill - Queen's University Press, 1978).

[Waterton Park], 1919. b&w. Camping trip, Marjorie Martin with Eber and Eva Foley. No known copies extant.

[Matador Ranch cattle], 1921. b&w. Moving herd from Swift Current, Saskatchewan area to U.S. No known copies extant.

[Pageant for Opening of Reconstruction of Kootenae House, Windermere, B.C.], 1922. David Thompson's Fort. No known copies extant.

[Skating on Bow River, Calgary], 1925. b&w. For Fox News. No known copies extant.

[Woman Exercising in Below Zero Weather, Calgary], 1925. b&w. In a bathing suit. For FN. No known copies extant.

[Captain Albert Carter Parachute Jumping, High River, Alberta], 1925. b&w. For FN. No known copies extant.

[Scenery around Lake Louise, Alberta], 1925. b&w. For FN. No known copies extant.

[Boy Scout Project, Calgary], 1925. b&w. Making and erecting birdhouses. For FN. No known copies extant.

[Roundup on Blacktail Ranch, Alberta], 1925. b&w. For FN. No known copies extant.

[Flight over Waterton Park], 1925. 35 mm. b&w. Includes views of Frank Slide. For FN. Copy in Fox Movietonews, N.Y.

[Great Asulkan Glacier, B.C.], 1926. 35 mm. b&w. For FN. Copy in Fox Movietonews, N.Y.

[Aerial Picture, High River, Alberta], 1926. b&w. Air base and area; cloud effects. For FN. No known copies extant.

[Rocky Mountains near Great Divide], 1926. b&w. For FN. No known copies extant.

[Snowfall in Canadian Rockies], 1926. 35 mm. b&w. 83′. Following exceptionally heavy snowfall. For FN. Copy in Fox Movietonews, N.Y.

[Parachute Jumping, High River], 1926. b&w. Captain A. Carter's first three students completing course. For FN. No known copies extant.

[Buffalo roundup, Wainwright Park, Alberta], May 1926. b&w. For FN. No known copies extant.

[Anniversary Celebration in Edmonton], 1926. b&w. For FN. For Alberta's 21st birthday. No known copies extant.

[Indian Sports Day in Banff], 1926. b&w. Probably Banff Indian Days. For FN. No known copies extant.

[Construction of Highway, Crow's Nest Pass], 1926. 35 mm. b&w. For FN. Copy in Fox Movietonews, N.Y.

[Buffalo Roundup, Wainwright], Dec. 1926. b&w. For FN. No known copies extant.

[Laying Deep Sea Cable, B.C.], 1927. b&w. Landing of cable at Bamfield. For FN. No known copies extant.

[Mildred Bennett on Sheep Ranch, Alberta], 1927. b&w. Sister of R. B. Bennet on P. Burns' Ranch. For FN. No known copies extant.

[Scenes in Rocky Mountains], 1927. b&w. For FN. No known copies extant.

[Buffalo Roundup, Wainwright], Dec. 1927. b&w. For FN. No known copies extant.

[Carnival Queens at Banff], 1928. b&w. Emily Mason and Mary Cross on dog team trip, Rockies. For FN. No known copies extant.

[Scenes at Carnival, Banff], 1928. b&w. For FN. No known copies extant.

[Scenes at Carnival, Jasper, Alberta], 1928. b&w. For FN. No known copies extant.

[Bird Sanctuary, Leduc, Alberta], 1928. b&w. For FN. No known copies extant.

[Governor General at Calgary Stampede], 1928. b&w. For FN. No known copies extant.

[Indians in Calgary area], 1928. b&w. For FN. No known copies extant.

[Caledonian Games], 1928. b&w. Featuring "the Young Ambassadors from the Old Country." For FN. No known copies extant.

[B.C. Mountaineering Club, Lake O'Hara area, B.C.], 1928. b&w. For FN. No known copies extant.

[Views of Rocky Mountains], c. 1926-28. b&w. Views Indians and tourists around Banff and Jasper. Copy in NFA.

[Turkey Farm at Ardenode, Alberta], 1928. b&w. Near Rockford, Alberta. For FN. No known copies extant.

[Celebration at Fort Saint James, B.C.], 1928. 35 mm. b&w. 100′. Enactment of arrival of Sir George Simpson, H.B.C., 1828. Copy in Fox Movietonews, N.Y.

[Tourists at Waterton Park], c. 1928. b&w. Featuring Marjorie Oliver, her sister-in-law, Jem Martin and Vic Valentine. To PB. No known copies extant.

"Sunshine Trails," 1929. 35 mm. b&w. Tourists from Great Falls traveling to Waterton and Banff. To PB. Copy in NFA (16 mm., 370′)

"Banff," 1929. 35 mm. b&w. c. 100′. Shows tourist attractions. To PB. Copy in NFA. (16 mm., 364′).

[Calgary Stampede], 1929. b&w. For FN. No known copies extant.

"Snow Time in the Rockies," c. 1920s. 35 mm. b&w. 700′. Sports in Banff National Park. To PB. Copies in NFA. (16 mm.) and NFB.

"Winter Wonderland," c. 1920s. 35 mm. b&w. c. 650′. Skiing in Banff National Park. Also 1936 version. To PB. Copies in NFA and NFB.

[Silk Trains across Canada], 1920s. b&w. No known copies extant.

"Home of the Buffalo," 1930. 35 mm. b&w. In Buffalo Park, Wainwright. For PB. Basis for sound version "The Return of the Buffalo," 1934. Copies in NFA and NFB. (also 16 mm. several copies, varying 300′ to 1275′).

"Sanctuary," 1930. b&w. Canadian wildlife taken late teens and twenties. For PB. No known copies extant.

"Through Mountain Gateways," 1930. b&w. Trip from Spokane, Washington, into Canadian Rockies. For PB. No known copies extant.

"Trails to the Wilderness," 1930. 35 mm. b&w. 1 reel. Saddle-pony trip, Jasper National Park - Tonquin Valley and Amethyst Lakes. For PB. Copies in NFA (16 mm., 400′) and NFB (16 mm., 350′).

"Good-bye to all That," 1930. 35 mm. b&w. 967′. Pack horse trip, Jasper to Mount Robson. For PB. Copies in NFA and NFB (16 mm., 330′), NFB and

PABC (2 prints, 35 mm.).

"New Skyscrapers for Old," 1931. 35 mm. b&w. c. 800'. Party from Toronto holidaying at Lake O'Hara, B.C. For PB. Copies in NFA (16 mm., 330'), NFB (16 mm., 300'), and PABC (35 mm.).

"Open Skyways in the Rockies," 1931. 35 mm. b&w. 1 reel. Motor trip from Banff to Golden. For PB. Copies in NFA (16 mm., 330'), and NFB (35 mm., 800').

[Construction of Big Bend Highway], c. 1931. b&w. West of Golden. For PB. No known copies extant.

"Here and There with the Birds of Canada," 1932. 35 mm. b&w. 1 reel. For PB. Copies in NFA (16 mm., 329') and NFB (16 mm., 338').

"Border Trails," 1932. b&w. Saddle pony trip along Waterton Lakes and Waterton-Glacier International Peace Park. For PB. No known copies extant.

"With Lure and Line in Jasper," 1932. 16 mm., b&w. 355'. Dr. J. G. Gunn, Calgary fishing in Maligne Lake. For PB. Also sound version "Sky Fishing." Copy in NFA.

"She Climbs to Conquer," 1932. 35 mm., b&w. Mountain climber Georgia Engelhard ascending Mount Victoria. For PB. Copy in NFA (16 mm., 640').

"The Beaver Family," 1932. 35 mm., b&w. 2 reels. Grey Owl and his beavers at Riding Mountain National Park, Man. For PB. Copy in NFA (16 mm., 594', 35 mm., 2 reels - c. 1545' and video cassette, 20 minutes).

"Grey Owl's Little Brother," 1932. 35 mm. b&w. 990'. sound. From "The Beaver Family" and "The Beaver People" (latter not taken by W. J. Oliver) Copies in NFA and NFB (also 16 mm., 394', and VRT cassettes, mainly 11 min.).

"Strange Doings in Beaverland," 1932. 35 mm. b&w. Grey Owl and beavers in P. A. National Park, Sask. For PB. Sound version produced, "Grey Owl's Strange Guests." Copies in NFA (16 mm. c. 372' and video cassette).

"Skiing at Lake Louise," 1933. 35 mm. b&w. For PB. Copies in NFA (16 mm., 350').

"Skiing in Cloudland," 1933. 35 mm. b&w. 829'. Showing Ptarmigan Valley to Deception Pass, Fossil Mountain. Party includes Peter and Catharine Whyte, Banff. For PB. Copies in NFA (also 16 mm., 327').

"Let's Go Skiing," 1933.[?] 16 mm. b&w. 373'. sound. Version of "Skiing in Cloudland."

"Sky Fishing," c. 1933. b&w. sound. Version of "With Lure and Line in Jasper." Copy in NFA [?].

"White Wings," 1933. 35 mm. b&w. 1 reel. Gulls along Vancouver coast in herring fishing season. For PB. Copy in NFA (16 mm., 290').

"Fleet Wings," 1933. 35 mm. b&w. 900'. Shows herring and ringbilled gulls and Caspian stern. For PB. Copies in NFA (also VTR, 10 min.).

"Cradle of Rivers," c. 1933. 35 mm. b&w. 877'. Pack horse trip. Banff to Jasper and over Columbia Icefields. For PB. Copies in NFA (also VTR, 10 min.).

"Hunting without a Gun," c. 1933. 35 mm. b&w. 1 reel. Wild animal views. For PB. Copy in NFA (16 mm., 252').

"Grey Owl's Strange Guests." 1934. 35 mm. b&w. c. 900'. sound. Version of "Strange Doings in Beaverland." Copies in NFA (various).

"Grey Owl's Neighbours," c. 1934. 35 mm. b&w. 875'. Grey Owl with birds and animals in P. A. National Park. For PB. Copies in NFA (16 mm., 75').

"Canada's Evergreen Playground," 1934. 35 mm. b&w. c. 800'. Featuring Victoria, B.C., and area. For PB and Victoria Island Publicity Bureau. Copies NFA (16 mm., 340') and PABC.

"Fishing for Tyee," 1934. 35 mm., b&w. c. 700'. Campbell River Fishing Club, B.C. catching tyee salmon. For PB. Copies in NFA (16 mm., c. 260'), NFA and PABC.

"Climbing Mount Tupper," 1934. 35 mm. b&w. 1 reel. In Glacier National Park. For PB. Sound version "The Game is Up." Copies in NFA and NFB.

"Stalking Big Game," 1934. 35 mm. b&w. Dan Byck, American hunter, and guide Jack Brewster camera hunting in Jasper area. For PB. Copies in NFA (16 mm., 400' and VTR, c. 11 min.).

"Waterton," 1934. 16 mm. b&w. 385'. Marjorie and Joan Oliver and Harold Long, Lethbridge, touring Waterton area. For PB. Copy in NFA.

"Birds: Rare and Fantastic," 1934. 35 mm. b&w. 1080'. Depicts red-throated loon and varieties of cormorants. For PB. Copies in NFA (also VTR, 10 min.) and NFB.

"Return of the Buffalo," 1934. 35 mm. b&w. 918'. sound. Mainly from "Home of the Buffalo." Copies in NFA (various) and NFB.

"Heart of the Rockies," c. 1934. b&w. 2 reels. Lake Louise to Jasper. Copy in NFA.

"Where Fighting Beauties Rise," 1935. 35 mm. b&w. c. 800'. Fly fishing for trout in Kamloops area, B.C. For PB. Copies in NFA (16 mm., 380'), NFB (16 mm., 378') and PABC (35 min.).

"Sunshine and Powder-Snow," c. 1935. 35 mm. b&w. Skiing in Sunshine Valley region. For PB. Copies in NFA (16 mm., and VTR, 10 min. 8 sec.).

"The Game is Up," 1935. 35 mm. b&w. sound. Version of "Climbing Mount Tupper." No known copies extant.

"Winter Wonderland," 1936. 16 mm. b&w. 279'. Skiing in Banff area. (Second film with this title.) For PB. Copy in NFA.

"Wild Life Ways," 1936. 35 mm. b&w. 1 reel. Canadian animals and birds in their natural habitat. For PB. Copies in NFA (16 mm., 400' and VTR, 11 min. 16 sec.).

"Angling in the Infinite," 1936. 16 mm. b&w. 312'. Joan Oliver and Swiss guides angling for trout in Marvel Lake, Banff National Park. For PB. Copy in NFA.

"Sea Lions of the Pacific," 1936. 35 mm. b&w. 1 reel. On rocky islands off n. tip of V.I. For PB. Copies in NFA (16 mm., 350', and VTR, 10 min.) and NFB (16 mm., 362').

"In the Shadow of Assiniboine," 1936. 35 mm. b&w. 1 reel. Joan Oliver and guide climbing Mount Wedgewood and viewing Assiniboine. For PB. Copies in NFA (16 mm., 345') and NFB (16 mm., 353').

"Hunter's Paradise," 1936. 35 mm. b&w. 1 reel. Hunting trip in Canadian Rockies. Jack Brewster's name included as co-director and co-photographer. For PB. Copy in NFB.

"Warriors of the Deep," 1936. 35 mm. b&w. M. Lerner catching swordfish off N.S. For PB and M. Lerner. Copies in NFA (16 mm., 345' and VTR, 9 min. 53 sec.).

"The Highlands of Cape Breton," 1937. 35 mm. b&w. Scenes along Cabot Trail. For PB. No known copies extant.

"Battling the Tuna," 1937. 35 mm. b&w. M. Lerner angling for tuna off N.S. coast. Copies in NFA (16 mm., 312' and VTR, 10 min.).

"By-Ways of Jasper," 1937. Short pack trips in Jasper National Park. For PB. No known copies extant.

"Jasper of the Lakes," 1938. 16 mm. b&w. 321'. Picturization of poem by T. P. O'Connor, Jasper. For PB. Copy in NFA.

"Colourful Days in Prince Albert National Park," 1938. 16 mm. color. Showing campfire and summer sports. For PB. No known copies extant.

[Airmail Service, Alberta], 1939. b&w. Trans-Canada Air Lines starting air mail service in Alberta. For CNR. No known copies extant.

"Banff to Lake Louise," c. 1939. 16 mm. color. Motor trip featuring scenery in Banff and Kootenay National Parks. For PB. No known copies extant.

"Pilgrims of the Wild," 1930s. 35 mm. b&w. A day with Grey Owl in P.A. National Park. For PB. No known copies extant.

"Fishing in the Rockies," 1930s. 35 mm. b&w. Fishing and camping. For PB. Copy in NFB.

"Over the Top of the Canadian Rockies," 1930s. b&w. Aerial views. No known copies extant.

"Where Cohoes Play," 1930s. Showing fighting qualities of coho salmon, B.C. For PB. No known copies extant.

"Health and Recreation in Prince Albert National Park," 1930s. b&w. Showing recreational attractions. For PB. No known copies extant.
"She Climbs to Conquer," 1930s. b&w. sound. Version of silent picture, same name.
"Saskatchewan's Scenic Lakeland," 1930s. b&w. Canoe trip through lakes in P.A. National Park. For PB. No known copies extant.
"Seeking Steelheads," 1930s. b&w. Catching steelhead trout in rivers of V.I. For PB. No known copies extant.
"The Game is Up," 1930s. b&w. sound. Version of "Climbing Mount Tupper." No known copies extant.
"The Trail to Jasper," 1930s. b&w. Views into Jasper via road from Edmonton. For PB. No known copies extant.
"Playgrounds of the Prairie," 1930s. b&w. Holidaying views in Riding Mountain National Park, Man. For PB. No known copies extant.
"Yoho," 1930s. b&w. Trail riders in Yoho National Park, B.C. For PB. No known copies extant.
"Trails of Jasper," 1930s. 16 mm. b&w. 450′. For PB. Copies in NFA and NFB.
"Summer Days at Waskesiu," 1930s. b&w. Holidaying in P.A. National Park. For PB. No known copies extant.
"Playgrounds of the Prairies," late 1930s. 16 mm. color. Holiday attractions of Riding Mountain National Park. For PB. No known copies extant.
"Playground of Two Nations," late 1930s. 16 mm. color. Holidaying in Waterton Park. For PB. No known copies extant.
[Ranch life], late 1930s. Harvesting, cattle, etc. taken on Diamond L Ranch, Millarville. No known copies extant.
"Playground Sanctuary," 1930s. Travel and wildlife in Elk Island National Park, Alberta. For PB. No known copies extant.
"Modern Voyageurs," c. 1930s. b&w. Travel through P.A. National Park's lake system. For PB. No known copies extant.
"Lakeland Resort," late 1930s or early 1940s. 16 mm. color. Recreational facilities at Sandy Beach, Astotin Lake, and Elk Island Park. For PB. No known copies extant.
"Sanctuary and Playground," late 1930s or early 1940s. 16 mm. color. Holidayers and wildlife in Elk Island Park. For PB. No known copies extant.
"Along the Cabot Trail," c. 1940. 16 mm. color. In Cape Breton Highlands National Park, N.S. For PB. No known copies extant.
"Lake Louise to Lac Beauvert," 1940. 16 mm. color. 720′. Motor trip from Lake Louise to Jasper. For PB. Copy in NFA.
[Mountain Trip], c. 1942. Doreen and A. J. Oliver traveling via Radium, Field, Yoho, etc. to Lake O'Hara. For PB. No known copies extant.
"Sea Rover's Summer," 1949. 35 mm. 1 reel. sound. From "Sea Lions of the Pacific." By Associated Screen News. Copy with United Artists.

W. J. Oliver produced an undetermined number of films depicting Michael and Helen Lerner on big game hunting expeditions in Africa, 1936-37, 1938, 1946-47; French Indo-China, 1938; Jasper area, Alberta and Northern B.C., 1937; Alaska, 1939 and 1940. The African and Indo-China films included sequence on life of native peoples, and considerable footage on all trips dealt with wildlife. The existence of any of above material has not been determined.

Commercial films which include footage taken by W. J. Oliver are:
"The Last Frontier," 1923. Produced by Ince Co., California.
"Calgary Stampede," 1925. Produced by Universal Jewel, California and starring Hoot Gibson.

Bill Oliver filming on Fossil Mountain, Banff National Park, 1932

Notes

A considerable amount of primary manuscript material relating to W. J. Oliver was available for use in the preparation of this book. The main items loaned by his family were: personal diaries, 1935-49, including detailed travel diaries and related papers which fully document the 1936-37 and 1937-38 African and Indo-China trips; a 60-page unpublished autobiographical manuscript; a small collection of correspondence; bulletins issued by Fox News, 1925-29; copies of speeches; a few miscellaneous items such as photographic equipment lists, telegrams, notebooks, etc. The Catharine Whyte Papers in the Archives of the Canadian Rockies, Banff, also contain a few Oliver letters. The Glenbow Archives holds a few original items and photocopies from the family. The writer's research papers, including tape recorded interviews will be housed in Glenbow's Archives.

Other sources include the *Calgary Herald* and the *Morning Albertan*, 1920s through 1940s; *Victoria Daily Times* and the Daily Province, Vancouver, 1930s; *The Country Guide*, December 1930; *Photography* (Cosmopolitan Press, London) October 1937; and *Canada's Weekly* (London) 1940 and 1946. The Oliver family made available a good collection of clippings. Among the valuable books consulted were: *A History of National Parks*, by W. F. Lothian (Ottawa: Parks Canada), and *Buffalo Bud*, by E. J. (Bud) Cotton and Ethel Mitchell (Vancouver: Hancock House, 1981). Other works which were critical sources for documenting the Oliver films have been detailed in the List of Films.

The majority of the photographs used in this book and in the Museum's exhibition are from the Oliver collection in the Glenbow Archives. This consists of approximately 2,150 original negatives which are comprised of a group purchased directly from E. W. Cadman who took over the W. J. Oliver Studio and two further collections obtained initially by the now defunct Horseman's Hall of Fame and Calgary Brewing and Malting Ltd., Calgary. In addition the Oliver family donated some forty original negatives to Glenbow and loaned quite a number of prints from which copy negatives have been made. The National Parks collection held by the National Photography Collection in the Public Archives in Ottawa includes a large proportion of original Oliver negatives and prints but as cataloguing is not completed these were largely unprobed. Parks Canada still holds a further group of views taken by Oliver while the photograph section of the Archives of the Canadian Rockies includes some of this photographer's views. In addition a large number of W. J. Oliver's photographs are held by members of his family.

I. AN EPIC MOMENT

1. Telegrams, 1936. W. J. Oliver Papers. (hereafter cited as W. J. O. papers.) In possession of Oliver family.
2. *Ibid.*
3. The Cabot Trail was built in 1932 by the Province of Nova Scotia. In 1936 the National Parks Branch upgraded the road, making some changes in route.
4. W. J. Oliver's diary, 19 July 1936. W. J. O. papers. (hereafter cited as W. J. O. diary.)
5. *Ibid.*, 7 August 1936. S. Kip Farrington, *Atlantic Game Fishing* (New York: Kennedy Bros. Inc., 1937.) 5. Farrington gives the date of this catch, a 462 lb. swordfish, as 3 August, however, as Oliver was present and recorded the event in his diary I have accepted his date.
6. *Ibid.*, 12 August 1936; Clipping file, Glenbow-Alberta Institute. (hereafter cited as Glenbow.); Farrington, *op. cit.*, 5. Again dates differ, Farrington citing 6 August. Other details substantially the same in all sources.
7. This movie, named "Warriors of the Deep," was a specially noted National Parks Branch production.
8. Farrington, *op. cit.*, 4-9.
9. "Battling the Tuna," as National Parks named this movie, also proved to be a particularly good and popular film.
10. Interview with Joan Cavers of Water Valley, 24-25 February, 1982.

II. THE BEGINNING

1. W.J. Oliver ms., 1 & 2. W.J.O. papers. (This, a 60-page unpublished autobiographical ms., typed, dealing mainly with filming experiences, is hereafter cited as W.J.O. ms.)
2. *Ibid.*, 2; Peter McDonald, "The Camera Artist of the 'Wild and Wooly'" *The Country Guide*, December 1930, 6.
3. W.JO. ms., 2 & 3.
4. *Calgary Herald*, 5 March 1910.
5. Bob Shields, ed. *Calgary, 1875-1975* (Calgary: Herald, 1974), 100.
6. *Calgary Herald*, 10 March 1910.
7. Max Foran, *Calgary: An Illustrated History* (Toronto: James Lorimer & Co. 1978), 76.
8. *Calgary Herald*, 75th Anniversary Issue, 6 September 1958, 4th Section, 22. Calgary's population is given for years 1875 to 1958, Dominion or City census figures where available, otherwise mainly Henderson's. For years 1909 to 1914 these are: 1909—29,265 (Police records); 1910—40,000 (Henderson's); 1911—43,704 (Dominion Census); 1912—73,759 (Henderson's); 1913—80,561 (Henderson's); 1914—81,161 (Henderson's). The 1910 figure is conservative when compared to estimates given by various other sources.
9. *Calgary Herald*, 11 April 1910.
10. *Ibid.*, 18 April 1910.
11. Immigrants from the British Isles and Europe formed the nucleus of the labour force and as indicated by the census of 1911 outnumbered Canadians. (See Foran, *op.cit.*, 84) These numbers plus the fact that many English immigrants adopted a critical attitude towards Canada and Canadian customs, resulted in this discriminatory attitude, despite the dominance of Anglo-Saxon backgrounds in the population.
12. See *Morning Albertan*, 7 March 1911.
13. *Calgary Herald*, 26 May 1913.
14. *Morning Albertan*, 17 April 1911. This ad does not give name of firm; applications were to be made to the clerk, Windsor Hotel—not an unusual procedure at the time. In W.J.O's ms. he states that he answered an Albertan ad for a photographer—this is the only such ad between 4 January to 13 June 1911; others appearing in the months before or after this date give information re advertiser and obviously do not apply.
15. Henderson's *Calgary City Director*, 1911. According to W.J.O. ms., Baynes was associated with Cooper. Albert B. Baynes, photographer, appears in Henderson's Calgary *Directory*, 1910, but is not listed in the 1911 *Directory* which appeared in October.
16. *Ibid.*
17. Ethel Heydon file, Glenbow Archives.
18. *Morning Albertan*, 14 October 1911. The bar was cleared at 8 feet 4½ inches. Frederick B. Turner, photographer, had roomed in the same house as F. B. Cooper in 1910, and probably was associated with Cooper's firm. This picture might have been taken about the time the *Albertan* made a formal arrangement with Bill.
19. Ibid., 22 November 1911.
20. See Oliver Album, ND-8-(171-2, 184), W. J. Oliver

Collection, Glenbow Archives.
21. W.J.O.'s ms., 5.
22. The *Albertan* during these years carried few local photos. Some clippings cite 1911 as the date when W.J.O. started his own business, however, facts regarding his activities indicate 1912, possibly early in the year; also, E.W. Cadman who bought the studio and had joined the business in 1923 always understood it commenced operation in 1912.
23. W.J.O. ms., 6.
24. *Calgary Herald*, 29 June 1912.
25. *Calgary Herald*, 3-9 September 1912; W. J. Oliver Photo Collection, Glenbow Archives.
26. *Ibid.*, 13 January 1913. W.J. Oliver Photo Collection, Glenbow, contains 14 photos of Burns fire, including the four that appeared in the *Herald*.
27. Grant MasEwan, *Calgary Cavalcade* (Saskatoon: Western Producer Book Services, 1975), 140.
28. *Ibid.*
29. *Calgary Herald*, 26 May 1913.
30. *Morning Albertan*, 21 May 1913.
31. W.J.O. ms., 14 & 15.
32. Interview with Dick Knights, Calgary, 5 May 1982; conversation with Freda McArthur (nee Knights) 7 May 1982.
33. *Ibid.*
34. *Calgary Herald*, 15 May 1914.
35. Frank W. Anderson, *Canada's Worst Mine Disaster* (Calgary: Frontier Publishing Ltd., c.1969), 15-37; *Calgary Herald*, 20 & 22 June 1914.
36. W.J.O. ms., 10 & 11.
37. *Calgary Herald*, 14 August 1914.
38. W.J.O. ms., 6. Norman S. Rankin was chief publicity commissioner of the Dept. of Natural Resources of the CPR. See *Albertan*, 4 March, 1912.
39. Normally Oliver's photographs for the CPR were commissioned or purchased and did not bear his stamp.
40. *Calgary Herald*, 23 February 1918; W.J.O. ms., 16 & 17.
41. *Ibid.*
42. *Ibid.*

III. OUTDOOR PHOTOGRAPHER

1. W.J.O. ms., 7.
2. *Ibid.*, 8; phone conversation with J.B. Cross, Okotoks, 12 November 1982.
3. *Calgary Herald*, 15 & 16 September 1919.
4. *Ibid.*, 18 September 1919. See also W.J.O. Photo Collection, Glenbow.
5. *Calgary Herald*, 25-30 August 1919.
6. Borein made an India ink sketch of a horse and rider in this position, then later an etching which he titled, "Scratching High," and a lithograph for the Calgary Stampede called, "I-See-You." Although Borein's use of Oliver's photograph has not been veritified his sketch closely resembles the photo.
7. W.J.O. ms., 5 & 12-14.
8. Interview with E. Walter Cadman, 10 February 1982.
9. Walter Meayers (Toppy) Edwards to S.S. Jameson, dated Sedona, Arizona, 14 August & 10 October 1982.
10. W.F. Lothian, *A. History of Canada's National Parks* (Ottawa: Parks Canada, 1981), Vol. IV, 137; W.F. Lothian to S.S. Jameson, 30 October 1982. The Parks Branch underwent numerous name changes over the years: Dominion Parks Branch, 1911-21; Canadian National Parks Branch, 1921-26; National Parks Branch, 1926-36; National Parks Bureau, 1936-50; National Parks Branch, 1950-73; Parks Canada, 1973 to present. To avoid confusion I am using the term Parks Branch throughout in this work.
11. W. .F. Lothian to S.S. Jameson, dated Ottawa, 20 October 1982.
12. Nemiskam National Park, including Chin and Fortymile Coulees, near Nimiskam, Alberta, was established in 1922 as an antelope reserve but by 1947 it was no longer required and so was abolished. Buffalo Park at Wainwright was established in 1908 and retained as a buffalo reserve until the area was taken over by the Department of National Defence in 1940. See W.F. Lothian, *A History of Canada's National Parks*, Vol. IV, 43-47 & 31-38.
13. Clipping, "Scene of Highway Ceremony Chosen," unidentified, Canadian Press, Ottawa, 23 December (1922), B.C. Provincial Archives.
14. Information from Marjorie Oliver, 20 April 1982.
15. McLaws, Redman, Lougheed, and Cairns Papers, 1910-1937, Glenbow Archives.
16. Interview, W. Cadman, 12 February 1982 & 30 May 1983.
17. *Ibid.*
18. *Ibid.*; Camera Equipment List. W.J.O. Papers.
19. Interview, W. Cadman, 12 February 1982. I am indepted to Walter Cadman for information re flash photography of the period.
20. W.J.O. ms., 17 & 18.
21. Interview, W. Cadman, 12 February 1982.

IV. MOVIE MAKING

1. J.W. Grant MacEwan, "The Matador Ranch," *Canadian Cattleman*, 2:4 (March 1940), 358; W.J.O. ms., 8 & 9.
2. *Canadian Cattleman*, 2:3 (December 1939).
3. Fox News file, W.J.O. papers.
4. W.J.O. ms., 16.
5. Fox News file.
6. Fox News file, Bulletin No. 279, 31 October, 1925.
7. *Ibid.*
8. W.J.O. ms., 19-20; Clipping file "Aeronautics—Canada," "First Alberta Air Base to go into Use Again," 7 October 1940. Glenbow Library.
9. See *Henderson's Province of Alberta Directory 1928-29* (Winnipeg: Henderson Directories, 1928), High River, p.391; Clipping file, *op.cit.*
10. *Calgary Herald*, 27 & 29 September 1924; *High River Times*, 2 October 1924.
11. Interview with Joan Cavers, 24-25 February 1982.
12. *Calgary Herald*, 17 October 1931.
13. *Ibid.* 4 May 1929.
14. *Ibid.*
15. *Calgary Herald*, 17 & 19 September 1930.
16. *Ibid.*, 18 & 19 September 1930.
17. *Calgary Herald*, 8 July 1950.
18. Interview with Walter Cadman, 12 February 1982.
19. Memo, Jack Maunder, Public Relations Officer to G.K. Nield, Montreal, 24 January 1948, & attached press release, 1945 (untitled), CPR Archives, Montreal.
20. Interview with W. Cadman, 12 February 1982; Interview with J. Cavers, 24 & 25 February 1982.
21. Interview with E.J. (Bud) Cotton, Calgary, 4 February 1982.
22. Courtney Ryley Cooper, 1886-1940, was an American writer mainly noted for his stories on the circus, the jungle, and life in the Canadian North-West.
23. W.F. Lothian, *A History of Canada's National Parks*, Vol. IV, 32-33.
24. W.J.O. ms., 32.
25. *Ibid.*, 32-33; *Calgary Herald*, 26 October & 10 November 1923. Article, "Camera-man Has Thrilling Experiences as Thousands of Buffalo Stampede Over Head," 10 November, includes photo showing movie directors with Bud Cotton and photographers Oliver and Perry in pit below them, heads and shoulders projecting.
26. W.J.O. ms., 34.
27. E.J. (Bud) Cotton with Ethel Mitchell, *Buffalo Bud* (Vancouver, B.C. & Blaine, Washington: Hancook House Publishers Ltd., 1981), 89.
28. W.J.O. ms., 34-35; Interview with Bud Cotton, 4 February 1982.
29. *Ibid.*; Interview with A.J. Langford, 17-22 April 1982.
30. Cotton & Mitchell, *op.cit.*, pp. 79-81; Interview with Bud Cotton, 4 February 1982.

31. This was part of film series "Canadian Cameo." "Home of the Buffalo" was deposited with Canadian Film Institute by Associated Screen News. See catalogue cards for both films—National Photography Collection, PAC.
32. Lothian, *op.cit.*, 34-35.
33. *Calgary Herald*, 12 October 1929.
34. Lothian, *op.cit.*, 138.
35. Lovat Dickson, *Wilderness Man: The Strange Story of Grey Owl* (Toronto: MacMillan of Canada, 1973), 204-7.
36. *Ibid.*; Lothian, *op.cit.*, 138.
37. W.J.O. ms., 37.
38. *Ibid.*
39. Grey Owl to Oliver, 5 April 1933. W.J.O. papers.
40. Peter Morris, *Embattled Shadows, A History of Canadian Cinema, 1895-1939* (Montreal: McGill—Queen's University Press, 1975), 172.
41. *Calgary Herald*, 14 May 1932.
42. *Ibid.* 23 July 1932.
43. W.J.O. ms., 16. Extent records of national parks films do not list W.J.O.'s 1919 Waterton Park picture, however a later version might include some of the footage; many earlier Parks Branch films are not now in existence.
44. W.J.O. ms., 20.
45. P. Norrish, *Embattled Shadows*, 170; W.J.O. ms. 26; Interview with F. Lothian, 20 April 1982.
46. W. Fergus Lothian to S. S. Jameson, 12 September 1983; interview with F. Lothian, 20 April 1982.
47. Lothian, *op.cit.*, 138. In a *Catalogue of Motion Pictures Films* (Ottawa: National Parks Bureau, 11943) of 85 films listed, 54 (63.5%) have been identified by W. F. Lothian as W. J. Oliver's works, also three other bird/bird and animal films undoubtedly contain footage taken by Oliver.
48. Interview with F. Lothian, 20 April 1982.
49. W.J.O. ms., 21.
50. Camera Lists and Data file, W.J.O. papers.
51. W.J.O. ms., 38-39. For description of a further Engelhard climb of Mount Victoria, 1933, see Georgia Engelhard, "The First Traverse of Mt. Victoria from South to North," *Canadian Alpine Journal*, 1934.
52. W.J.O. ms., 39.
53. *Ibid.*, 29 & 30.
54. *Ibid.*, 30 & 31.
55. *Ibid.*, 47-48.
56. *Ibid.*, 42-47.
57. Catharine Whyte Papers, Archives of the Canadian Rockies, Banff.
58. S.C. Cain, "'Ski-Camering' up where the Snow Burns," *Calgary Herald*, 14 May 1932.
59. W.J.O. ms., 31.
60. *Calgary Herald*, 29 August 1928.
61. *Ibid.*
62. Interview with Joan Cavers, 24-25 February 1982.
63. W. J. Oliver to Joan Oliver, dated Louisbourg, N.S., 5 August 1936. Joan Caver's personal papers. (In her possession.)
64. Interview with A. J. Langford, 17-22 April 1982. Information from A. J. Oliver's diary of trip, 1941. A. J. Langford's personal papers. (In her possession); D. Huffman, Notes, 25 August 1982.
65. *Calgary Herald*, 3 October 1925.
66. National Photography Collection, Parks Department Photograph Collection, Public Archives of Canada, Ottawa.
67. W.J.O. ms., 41-42.
68. *Calgary Albertan*,27 June 1940.
69. Interview with F. Lothian, 20 April 1982.
70. W.J.O., ms., 39-40.
71. Interview with Joan Cavers, 24-25 February 1982. A copy of the poem is included in Joan Cavers' papers, Glenbow Archives.
72. Clipping, "U.S. Joins Canada in Paying Tribute to David Thompson," unidentified, n.d. Provincial Archives of B.C.; also, *Cranbrook Courier*, 8 September 1922, refers to ceremony being "well filmed and photographed." *Golden Star*, 8 September 1922 notes that Oliver was in attendance. I am indebted to David Mattison, Sound and Moving Image Division, PABC for the above references. A photo taken at the dedication of the memorial fort shows two cinematographers on roof of building. The man wearing plus fours was probably W.J.O. as this was his usual mode of dress at this time.
73. W.J.O. diary, 23 May - 2 June 1935.
74. *Comox District Free Press*, 5 May 1949.
75. *Daily Province*, Vancouver, 10 June 1931.
76. *Comox Argus*, Courtenay, B.C. 11 June 1931.
77. F. Lothian to S. S. Jameson, 12 September 1983.
78. W.J.O. diary, 5-20 June 1935; W.J.O. ms., 50-51; *The Daily Province*, Vancouver, 13 July 1935; clipping, "Doesn't Fake His Scenes," unidentified, n.d. W.J.O. papers.
79. P. Norrish, *Embattled Shadows*, 172.
80. Interview with W. Cadman, 12 February 1982.
81. Interview with Joan Cavers, 24-25 February 1982.
82. F. Lothian to S. S. Jameson, 12 September, 1983.
83. Telegram, Robert J.C. Stead to W. J. Oliver, 2 August 1937. W.J.O. papers.
84. Interview with Joan Cavers, 24-25 February 1982. National Parks Bureau Catalogue of Motion Pictures Films, 1943, lists 8 W.J.O. films, 16 mm., colour.
85. F. Lothian to S. S. Jameson, 20 October 1982.
86. Lothian, *History of Canada's National Parks*, Vol. IV, 138.

V. RANCHING AND SAFARIS

1. The purchase from Clinton J. Ford consisted of: W.½ of S.5, S.E.¼ of Sec. 7, the part of N.E.¼ of S.7 lying south of N. Fork of Sheep Creek, N.E.¼ of S.6 & W.½ of S.8, all of T.21, R.2, W.-5. The M.T. Millar land was N.W. ¼ of S.7 and the N.E. ¼ of S.7 lying north of the North Fork of Sheep River. From Land Titles Office, Calgary.
2. Roy Flieger, "The Royalite Camp," *In the Light of the Flares: History of Turner Valley Oilfields* (Turner Valley, Alberta: Sheep River Historical Society, 1979), 30.
3. H. G. Pallister, Co-ordinator, Regulatory Service, Animal Industry Division, Alberta Agriculture to S. S. Jameson, dated Stettler, Alberta, 6 December 1983. The LIV brand was allowed to expire 1937. The Diamond L was transferred to F. E. Gourlay, November 1949. See also *Alberta Horse Cattle & Sheep Brands* (Edmonton: Dept. of Agriculture, 1937). No brand book was printed between 1925 & 1937.
4. W.J.O. diary, 1935.
5. *Annual Report of the Department of Public Works of the Province of Alberta*, 1933-34 (Edmonton: W. D. McLean, King's Printer, 1934), 12.
6. W. J. Oliver to Joan, *S.S. Normandie* on Atlantic Ocean, n.d. "Spike" was Oliver's nickname for Doreen.
7. Most of the information contained in this chapter was obtained through interviews, letters and notes from the three Oliver girls, Joan Cavers, Doreen Huffman and Audrey Jean Langford, reinforced by the author's own memories when living on a neighbouring ranch at Millarville.
8. W.J.O. travel diary, 1936-37, 18-25 November 1936. Unless otherwise noted W.J.O. travel diary, 1936-37, 14 November 1936 - 3 March 1937, is the source of information concerning this expedition.
9. *Albertan*, Calgary, 4 May 1937.
10. *Calgary Herald*, 4 September 1937.
11. Interview with Jack Holroyd, 23 August 1983.
12. *Calgary Herald*, 4 September 1937.
13. *Ibid.*
14. *Ibid.*
15. See for example clipping "A Photographer of Animals," unidentified, n.d. W.J.O. papers.
16. *Calgary Herald*, *op.cit.*
17. W.J.O. diary, 7 September 1937.
18. W.J.O. diary, 15 December 1937 - 10 April 1938. As Indo—China consists of Vietnam, Laos, and

Cambodia, many of the places mentioned became widely known during the Indo-China and Vietnam wars.
19. Script of talk beginning "Look at the Map of Asia. . . ." n.d. W.J.O. papers.
20. W.J.O diary, *op.cit.*
21. Script of talk, "The Hunt at Ban-Me-Thout, 20-25 March 1938." W.J.O. papers.
22. *Calgary Albertan*, 21 March 1939.
23. W.J.O. diary, 16 April - 30 May 1938.
24. *Albertan*, Calgary, 4 May 1937. See also W.J.O. travel diary, 14 December 1936 - 19 February 1937 & W.J.O. diary, 25 April - 28 May 1938.
25. *Albertan*, *Ibid.*
26. W.J.O. to Joan, dated Sheep Camp, Indian River, Kenai Peninsula, Alaska, 2 October 1939.

VI. RUSTLE OF ASPEN LEAVES

1. W.H. Corkhill, "As the Crane Flies," *Canada's Weekly*, 29 March 1940. (Probably published in London by the Canadian government.)
2. Harper, Cory, "W. J. Oliver, Cameraman to Naturalist," *Photography* (London: Cosmopolitan Press Ltd.) Vol. VI, No. 62, October 1937, p.6.
3. W.J.O. diary, 22 July - 29 August 1946.
4. *Ibid.*, 29 October 1946.
5. Clipping, "Party Leaves for Africa," unidentified, n.d. (Information contained therein indicates the 1946-47 trip.) W.J.O. papers. Also, Marie Elwood, Chief Curator of History, Nova Scotia Museum, Halifax, to S.S. Jameson, 29 July 1982. The expedition produced controversy in Halifax concerning the appropriateness of the specimens and the expense incurred.
6. *Calgary Herald*, 28 February 1947.
7. *Market Examiner*, Calgary, 1 March 1945.
8. *Ibid.*, 25 March 1948. Steers in the 1948 shipment averaged 1,035 lbs. and brought $16.15 per cwt., heifers averaged 950 lbs. at $15.35.
9. *Calgary Herald*, 28 October 1949. See also 3 October 1949 re sale of property.
10. W.J.O. to Joan Oliver, dated Shelburne, N.S., 31 August 1936.
11. Description of calendar picture, "Bow Lake—Banff-Jasper Highway—Reproduced from a photograph by W. J. Oliver," n.d., (writer unidentified). Joan Cavers papers. The view of Bow Lake with marvellous mountain reflections features a white tipi to the right and a deer in the foreground eyeing it with interest—an appealing, lovely scene.
12. Julia Day, "On Being an Accomplished Photographer," *Albertan Magazine* (Edmonton: Kingsway Publishing Western Ltd.,), July/August, 1982, p.18.
13. W.H. Corkhill, "As the Crane Flies," *Canada's Weekly*, 29 March 1940.
14. W.J.O. script of talk for CBC., beginning "For Real Sport. . .," untitled, undated. He notes that a hunter could shoot an animal from a distance of one hundred to three hundred yards while the photographer had to reduce that distance considerably. His own camera shots normally were from distances of 25 feet to 100 feet. Also, he believed that "telephoto lenses should be used only when you cannot stalk close enough to your subject to obtain a large object on the film." W.J.O. ms., 58.

Vessel plying coastal waters, Maritimes, 1936

Index

Photo Sources

Photographs of Bill Oliver were taken by a number of people, including Walter Cadman, members of the Oliver family, and the view on page 50 by E. J. "Bud" Cotton. Wherever possible, Oliver prints for this book were made from original negatives, but in some instances, the negative was lost and copies had to be made by Ron Marsh and his staff in Glenbow's Photography Department.

Sources are as follows:

Archives of the Canadian Rockies, Banff: p. 24 (PB-129), p. 41 (PD-49-1-372), and p. 134 (NA-66-1767).

National Photography Collection, Public Archives of Canada, Ottawa: p. 55 top (C-36186), p. 65 (PA-804269), and p. 73 (PA-804004).

The Oliver Family (Mrs. Marjorie B. Oliver, Joan Cavers, Doreen Huffman, and Audrey Jean Langord): pp. 8, 11, 13, 19, 23, 29, 43, 44, 46, 49 bottom, 50, 55 bottom, 57, 60-61, 62, 66 left, 66 right, 68, 72, 76, 81, 82 (all four), 85, 87, 89, 90, 91, 92, 95, 101, 116 left, 116 right, 126 left, 126 right, 130, 131, and 133.

Parks Canada, Ottawa: pp. 7, 10, 53, 58, 59, 71 left, 71 right, 105, 127, 128 left, 128 right, 129, 145, 146, and 147.

Glenbow Archives, Calgary: p. 5 (NBH-16-303), p. 15 (ND-8-268), p. 17 (NB-16-505), p. 17 (NB-16-519), p. 21 (NB-16-498), pp. 26-27 (NB-16-600), p. 31 (NB-16-260), p. 32 (NB-16-2), p. 33 (NB-16-149), p. 35 (NBH-16-91), p. 36 (NBH-16-48), p. 37 (NBH-16-231), p. 39 (ND-8-209), p. 47 (NBH-16-491), p. 49 top (NB-16-331), p. 50 upper right (NB-16-328), p. 50 lower right (NB-16-322), p. 74 (NB-16-263), p. 78 (NBH-16-472), p. 97 (ND-8-260), p. 98 (ND-8-174), p. 108 (NB-16-595), p. 109 (ND-8-4), p. 110 left (NB-16-587), p. 110 right (NB-16-589), p. 111 (NB-16-55), p. 112 (NB-16-324), p. 117 (NB-16-465), p. 118 (NB-16-480), p. 119 (NB-16-448), p. 120 (NB-16-524), p. 121 (NB-16-528), p. 122 (NB-16-381), p. 123 (ND-8-423), p. 124 (ND-8-157), p. 125 (ND-8-176), p. 132 (ND-8-506), 134 right (ND-8-33), p. 135 (NBH-16-457), p. 136 (NBH-16-455), p. 137 (NB-16-158), p. 138 (NBH-16-463), p. 139 (NBH-16-280), p. 140 (NBH-16-116), p. 141 top (NBH-16-168), p. 141 bottom (NBH-16-17), p. 142 top (NBH-16-97), p. 142 bottom (NBH-16-243), p. 143 (NBH-16-56), and p. 144 (ND-8-92).

A Portfolio of Oliver Photographs

The Indians

 Sarcee Indians at Calgary, in the teens

Indian camp at Calgary for the Royal Visit, 1939

Wife and daughter of Big Knife, Sarcee Indians, 1911

Two Young Men and daughter, Sarcee Indians, 1911

Banff Indian Days, 1919

Sarcee Indians in first Calgary Stampede parade, 1912

Sweatlodge frame for the Sarcee Sun Dance, 1911. The buffalo skull was an altar piece while the paddle at right was used for carrying hot stones for the ritual.

Indian at the Calgary Stampede, ca.1920s

Indians in Calgary Stampede parade, ca.1912

Man with his grandson, northern Saskatchewan, ca.1930s

Mrs. Lavallee preparing sinew threads, northern Saskatchewan, ca.1930s

Calgary and District

Accident in Calgary, 1920. An early morning streetcar encountered icy tracks on Mount Royal Hill and ploughed into a drug store at 17th Avenue and 14th Street S.W.

Josie Welsh on *Kickaroo*, 1923. The horse held the high jumping record of seven feet four inches in his class.

Destruction of the Sherman Rink, Calgary, 1915

Car races at the Calgary Exhibition, 1918

Hill climb, Calgary, in the teens

Glen House's championship team, 1925. With driver Slim Moorehouse, a team of thirty-two horses drawing eight wagons was a feature attraction of the Calgary Stampede.

Turner Valley oilfields, 1929

Dryland farm near Nobleford, 1925

An ocean of stooks near Vulcan, 1928

Rocky Mountains

Climbing the Needles above Lake Louise, 1936. Joan Oliver and guide Chris Hasler practise for an ascent of Mount Wedgewood.

Bill Oliver in camp, ca.1930s

Waterton Lakes, 1934

Mount Lefroy and Lake O'Hara, Yoho National Park

Riders overlooking Pass Creek, Waterton National Park, ca.1930s

Crowfoot Glacier, Banff National Park, ca.1934. This photograph was taken before construction of the Banff-Jasper Highway.

Setting up camp, Waterton National Park, 1934. Harold Long, Marjorie and Joan Oliver.

Rock Island Lake, Mount Assiniboine Provincial Park, B.C., 1936

Skiers at Banff Winter Carnival, 1930. Left to right: Mary Cross (later Mrs. Mary Dover), unknown, and Emily Mason.

Pack train in the high country

Burgess Mountain, above Emerald Lake, in Yoho National Park

Walter Nixon, Banff guide

Ranching and Rodeo

Branding time, ca.1920s

The camp cook at roundup time, ca.1920s

Rancher George Lane, 1919

Cattle being dipped to prevent mange, ca.1920s

Contestants at the Calgary Stampede, ca.1930s

Steer decorating, Calgary Stampede, 1936

Frank Sharpe on *Cyclone*, Calgary Stampede, ca.1930s

Calf roping, Calgary Stampede, 1936

Herman Linder on *Easy Money*, Calgary Stampede, ca.1930s

Wild horse race, Calgary Stampede, ca.1930s

Cyril Gates on *Diggin's Papoose*, Calgary Stampede, ca.1930s

Horse roundup near Hussar, ca.1919

Scenes

View of Cabot Trail, Cape Breton, 1936

Ernest Feuz, Swiss guide, on the peak of Mount Victoria, 193

Ruins of Louisbourg, 1936